"Secure in Christ"

Connie Becker

GOD'S
Magnificent Plan

HOW IT'S DESIGNED AND WHY IT WORKS

Connie Becker

WestBow Press
A DIVISION OF THOMAS NELSON
& ZONDERVAN

Copyright © 2014 Connie Becker.

All rights reserved. No part of this book may be used or reproduced by any means, graphic, electronic, or mechanical, including photocopying, recording, taping or by any information storage retrieval system without the written permission of the publisher except in the case of brief quotations embodied in critical articles and reviews.

Scripture verses indicated as having come from The Living Bible are taken The Living Bible, Paraphrased. Copyright © 1975 by Tyndale House Publishers. All rights reserved.

Unless otherwise indicated, Scripture verses are taken from the Holy Bible, New International Version®, NIV®. Copyright © 1973, 1978, 1984, 2011 by International Bible Society. Used by permission of Zondervan. All rights reserved.

WestBow Press books may be ordered through booksellers or by contacting:

WestBow Press
A Division of Thomas Nelson & Zondervan
1663 Liberty Drive
Bloomington, IN 47403
www.westbowpress.com
1 (866) 928-1240

Because of the dynamic nature of the Internet, any web addresses or links contained in this book may have changed since publication and may no longer be valid. The views expressed in this work are solely those of the author and do not necessarily reflect the views of the publisher, and the publisher hereby disclaims any responsibility for them.

Any people depicted in stock imagery provided by Thinkstock are models, and such images are being used for illustrative purposes only. Certain stock imagery © Thinkstock.

ISBN: 978-1-4908-5016-0 (sc)
ISBN: 978-1-4908-5017-7 (hc)
ISBN: 978-1-4908-5015-3 (e)

Library of Congress Control Number: 2014915898

Printed in the United States of America.

WestBow Press rev. date: 09/25/2014

CONTENTS

Acknowledgements vii
Introduction: My Story ix

Section One: God's Dilemma

Chapter 1: The Things That God Cannot Do 3
Chapter 2: The Spiritual Realm's Rebellion 9
Chapter 3: The Ultimate Purpose of the Natural-Realm World 23
Chapter 4: Creation: Part One of God's Plan of Salvation 39
Chapter 5: Created in the Image of God 43
Chapter 6: The Fall of Humanity 61

Section Two: God's Solution

Chapter 7: The Role of the Body in the Plan of Salvation 79
Chapter 8: What Is So Special about Jesus? 89

Chapter 9: Jesus Is the Ark of the Covenant 97
Chapter 10: The Vehicle of the Cross 115
Chapter 11: Putting the Plan of Salvation into Action 129

Section Three: The Certainty of Salvation

Chapter 12: The Certainty of Salvation 147
Chapter 13: Everything Changes 155
Chapter 14: Living Under the New Covenant of
              Grace 179
Chapter 15: My Adventures in the Scriptures 211
Chapter 16: Can a Christian Lose His or Her
              Salvation? 233
Chapter 17: The Inheritance of the Second Birth........247

Sources..265

ACKNOWLEDGEMENTS

All gratitude and praise to God the Father, God the Son, and God the Holy Spirit, the one true author and finisher of our faith.

INTRODUCTION: MY STORY

We all experience events that instantly change our lives or have moments when a light turns on in our minds, giving us a new understanding or perspective. Then there are moments when our lives change suddenly and drastically and we are sent into a completely new reality. These events and moments can be wonderful blessings that bring happiness and success, or they may be devastating occurrences that plunge us into a nightmare that threatens the very foundation of our lives. As human beings, we are, by nature, resistant to change, so the realization that our lives can be instantaneously altered is often a source of fear and insecurity. This book is the result of my personal journey to find security and peace in a turbulent world that offers neither.

    I have had many wonderful moments of enlightenment, and many beautiful events have blessed my life. I am very grateful for each one. However, it is the devastating blows, the ones that sent me reeling and shook me to my very core, that led me to seek the Lord and find the greatest blessings of all. I suffered two major events, both of which caused the bottom to fall out of my life and sent me on a desperate search for answers.

My First Devastating Event

I look back on my life before the first devastating blow as if it were a wonderful fairy tale. We were a happy, carefree family, full of love and laughter. I had parents who loved each other and doted on us kids. I know we weren't rich, but it seems to me that we were because we had everything we wanted. These were fun-filled, magical years, and I am so blessed to have had them. Still, I remember one day as I walked home from school when a fearful thought came into my mind: *What if one of us got very sick and couldn't afford to go to the hospital?* My next thought was more powerful than the first: *Oh, my dad would do something.* That completely settled the matter in my mind. I knew that my dad would do anything for us; I was totally secure in that knowledge.

It was in the fall after I turned fourteen that everything changed. Everyone in my family except for me had gone to a birthday party for one of my aunts. I returned home before everyone else did just in time to watch them laughing and joking as they walked up to the house. Dad was carrying one of the younger kids on his shoulders. It was obvious that my family had a great time at the party. Looking at them at that moment, no one could have predicted that in less than an hour, my thirty-six-year-old father would be lying on our living room floor dead from a massive heart attack.

Our lives were suddenly plunged into a tragic new reality. I felt like Alice falling into the rabbit hole. We were sent reeling into a dark place that was full of grief and pain. It was a place of sadness and heartache with no visible way out and no hope that anything would ever be the same again. I don't remember much about the first year except that we lived in a state of slow motion and numbness. We looked normal and went through the motions of life, but we weren't normal. Much looked the same, but nothing was the same. We were traumatized souls shaken to the very core of our being.

Our plight got worse before it got better. As the shock and numbness wore off, the pain and sadness intensified. My heartbroken mother was left with a house, a small income, and four children (I was the eldest). To make matters worse, we were no longer four happy, carefree children; we were hurting, lonely, damaged children. The problems just kept coming. I have always thought that our story would make a wonderful novel. If I had any idea how to write one, I would—and my mother would be the heroine of the story, because that is exactly the part she played. She held us together, nursed our wounds, and faced each problem as it came along. The odds were stacked against us, but we slowly built a new life together.

It was during this time of rebuilding our lives that I started the habit of suppressing my emotions and pain. At fourteen years old, I had learned well the high cost of loving someone. I missed my dad so much that my heart ached with loneliness. My memories of him became an exercise in pain and grief. To get to those good memories, I had to go through a wall of pain, so I simply stuffed the pain and tried not to remember. The truth is that I wanted to scream at the top of my lungs, "All I want is my dad back!" But death is among those things that cannot be changed, so I was left to cope with problems I could not fix.

My teenage years became a nightmare. While my friends were happily caught up in teenager stuff, I began contemplating questions for which I had no answers. These issues haunted me and were often the last thing I thought about before I fell asleep at night. Why did God allow the man who was murdering children in our community to live while he let my loving dad die? Why would God let us be hurt like this? Did we do something to deserve what happened? Where was my dad? Was he in heaven, was he suffering in some awful place, or was he simply lying in that horrible grave? These kinds of questions swirled around in my head, so I stopped looking for answers and stuffed the questions down into my soul along with the other things I could not fix.

Where there is hurt and pain, there is anger. I was full of anger. Usually when we are angry, we can focus that anger on the one who harmed us. It felt to me as if I had no one to blame for my anger and no way to get rid of it. I had been deserted by my dad, but it certainly wasn't something he had done on purpose. I could have blamed God and been angry with Him, but at that time, I was too frightened of what He might do to admit I was angry with Him. So, I did what I was getting very good at doing: stuffing my anger down into my soul and holding it there.

The one thing I could not stuff was the fact that I had lost my ability to trust. I didn't trust God and I no longer trusted myself. I had made some heartbreaking decisions the year after Dad died, and my confidence in myself had been badly shaken. As far as I was concerned, every moment held within it the potential for disaster, so I lived in fear, waiting for the next awful thing to happen. I knew I would not survive another tragedy, so I began the futile practice of trying to control those things that are uncontrollable.

I could not have expressed my struggles back then because I wasn't behaving consciously. I was simply doing the best I could. Moving on into my adult life, I married a wonderful, loving man. We had two beautiful little girls. Surprisingly, these years were a lot like my early childhood, full of love and laughter. The only difference was my inner battle with fear, anger, and the need to try to protect my loved ones from harm so I would not lose them. I became an overprotective mother and wife, living in constant fear that something or someone would snatch my loved ones away. I had no idea what all this was doing to me or the amount of energy I was using just trying to live a normal life.

My Second Shocking Episode

During my early thirties, the day finally came when I lost the ability to cope and the bottom fell out of my life for the second time. All the years of carrying a load of worry and fear, grief, anger, guilt, and shame sent me spiraling into mental turmoil, initiating a spiritual battle that changed my life forever. When the bottom fell out of my life the first time, I was sent into a dark place full of grief and pain. The second time, it seemed as if I were instantly hurled into a place of absolute horror where I could sense the very presence of evil.

In one shocking moment, my mind turned against me. Even worse, it turned against God in a most vile and uncontrollable way. I was leisurely reading an article in a Christian magazine that mentioned an unforgivable sin known as blasphemy of the Holy Spirit. I had always been taught that there was no sin that God would not forgive, so I reached for my Bible and looked up the Scriptures mentioned in the article. It was at the very moment I read those Scriptures that my soul was shaken to its core. My mind filled with horrible thought-attacks directed at God, things I personally would never have wanted to think or say. Then the accusations started—that I had committed the unpardonable sin and had forever lost my salvation in Christ. I didn't know what was happening to me or why, and I could do nothing to stop it. The longer I fought against the wild thoughts, the more tired I became as depression and fear took hold of my mind. I became more and more distressed until I could hardly eat. Every waking moment was torture.

I never received a clear diagnosis for my mental condition. The closest I can come to describing it is to say that I had clinical depression aggravated by fear, along with a strong thought disorder most likely brought on by post-traumatic stress. This, of course, is a composite diagnosis of my own making. I have no idea what a professional would have labeled my mental state. I went to a psychologist for a short time and took antidepressants for a number of months, but it didn't take me long to discover that, as helpful as these methods can be for others, they were not going to help me find my answers. I had already come to realize that my problems were not confined to my mind alone but involved deeper spiritual issues, as well.

Sometime before my mental breakdown, I happened to watch a daytime talk show. The topic for that day was a strange one. It focused on people whose spiritual and religious beliefs caused them to have mental turmoil and breakdowns. The show featured people suffering from this problem as well as professionals who were trying to help them. The professionals' final comments were that there was very little they could do to help people with these kinds of problems. Although I sympathized with the unfortunate souls, I could not imagine how they got into that position. At that moment, I had no way of knowing that in the not too distant future, I would be joining their ranks.

As the saying goes, I found myself between a rock and a hard place. I truly believed it was possible that I had somehow or in some way committed some unforgivable sin. I even had times when I was unsure that I had ever been saved at all. I could not coherently deal with my spiritual-belief issues because of my mental condition. At the same time, I could not help my mental turmoil because my spiritual battle was feeding the depression and fear that had overtaken my mind. For months, I looked for help in many places. I ran to a Christian psychologist, my family doctor, a variety of pastors, my family and friends, and pretty much anybody who would listen to me. I was desperately trying to find someone who would have an answer or give me some magic pill. I was hoping to pop out of my mental mess as quickly as I had fallen into it, but nothing I tried gave me any lasting relief. My question became, *where does one go for help with spiritual and religious beliefs issues?*

Then one day, my family doctor said to me that I was welcome to come see him whenever I needed, but there was nothing more he could do for me. I left his office knowing I was out of options. The only hope left for me was to receive a miracle. I thought the chances for that were very slim, indeed. I had been crying out to the Lord for help from the instant I was plunged into this madness. There had been moments when I could sense His presence with me, but the battle in my mind always overtook the love and peace that I experienced in those fleeting seconds. When I returned home from the doctor's that day, the house was quiet and empty. I got down on my knees and prayed. "Lord, I quit. Nothing I do is working, and no one is able to help me. I choose you to be my physician and my psychologist. If I get well, it will be because you make me well." This was the turning point. I had just enlisted the greatest psychologist the world has ever known, the Creator of my soul, asking Him to take complete control over my destiny. You might be thinking that I got off my knees that day with a quiet mind, all healthy and whole, but that is not the kind of miracle I received. Instead, the Lord led me out of my dilemma one laborious step at a time.

It would be nearly three years before I was sure I would survive at all. Those were the most difficult years of my life; however, they were also the three most glorious years of my life. I would not want to go through that time again, but I am so very grateful and feel privileged to have experienced it. The Holy Spirit taught me how to deal with every aspect of the problems in my mind and in my spirit. During those years, I would think to myself that if the Lord would simply take away those horrific thought-attacks, then my mind would heal. Those attacks gradually became fewer and much less powerful, and my mind did heal, not because He instantaneously healed me, but because He taught me how to defeat them so they no longer had any power over me.

The truth is that my biggest problems came from my ingrained misconceptions about God and my inability to trust Him. These are belief problems that the Lord does not just instantly change or magically zap away. I was a believer and had already accepted Jesus as my Savior long before this happened to me. However, I did not know Him very well, nor did I understand how His gift of salvation worked. Those are the things I came to know as the Lord led me out of my despair. He gave me the courage to once again open the Holy Bible and begin to study His Word. As I obeyed Him in this, He gave me the gift of revelation and I began to understand how great a salvation we have in Christ Jesus.

Conclusion

This is not a book about learning how to walk out of mental turmoil; instead, it is a book about having a firm foundation in Christ Jesus and expanding our understanding of salvation. For many years, I have taught Bible studies and listened to many discussions between Christians. It is all too common for sincere Christians to be doubtful about their standing in Christ. And, all too often, we cannot explain why we believe that Jesus is the Savior of the world. It is true that we do not have to have a complete understanding to accept Christ and have our salvation in Him. If that were a requirement, then none of us would ever be saved. As it is sometimes said, "You don't have to know how a car is put together to be able to drive it." However, if you are going to take care of it and keep it running well, then you need to have some knowledge of how it works. Salvation is like that. We don't have to fully understand it to accept our salvation from the Lord, for it is a gift full of wonderful mysteries. Nevertheless, if we want to live more fully in the blessings of our salvation and have it be a solid, working part of our lives while we are here on Earth, then we need a foundation to understand how salvation operates.

I come from a family of mechanically gifted people. As a child, I believed that my dad and uncles could fix anything. They always seemed to be in the process of learning how something worked, especially cars and machinery. If I close my eyes, I can see those dear men with their heads under the hood of some car, discussing its mechanics. I sometimes think I inherited their need to understand how things work. I joke when I say that I see myself as a kind of spiritual mechanic. Over many years, I have spent a great deal of time trying to figure out the mechanics of God's plan for the salvation of humankind. So, I invite you to figuratively put your head under the hood with me as we seek to understand just how and why the sacrifice of Christ Jesus worked for the salvation of humankind.

Section One
GOD'S DILEMMA

CHAPTER 1

THE THINGS THAT GOD CANNOT DO

When I was a child, I couldn't understand why God didn't simply declare us to be forgiven. My reasoning was that He is God and can do anything He wants to do. While it is true that God is sovereign, it is also true that if He wanted to provide a way for the salvation of humanity, then He had some major obstacles to overcome. It was during one of those sweet moments of revelation when I finally came to realize that there are things God cannot do. If we hope to gain a better understanding of God's plan for the salvation of humankind and of why He reacted to Adam and Eve as He did, then we must first grasp the fact that there are things God cannot do. These things are among His biggest obstacles to reuniting Himself with humankind, which is the ultimate objective of salvation.

Obstacle One
(Relevant Scriptures: Ezra 9:15; Revelation 21:22–27; Ezekiel 1:4–28; Exodus 3:1–6, 13:21, 19:16–25, 33:18–23)

The first and most important thing that God cannot do is change the fact that He is holy. It is His holiness that makes it impossible for Him to come in direct contact with sin. Even worse, He cannot come into direct contact with those things that are simply imperfect. His holiness and glory automatically destroy sin or imperfection if it comes into His full and direct presence. There is nothing that God can do about it except separate Himself from it. Ezra declares to God, "O Lord, God of Israel, you are righteous! Here we are before you in our guilt, though because of it not one of us can stand in your presence" (Ezra 9:15).

In the Old Testament stories, God never allowed anyone to come directly into contact with His powerful presence. He concealed Himself in a burning bush; He hid in a cloud by day and in a pillar of fire by night as He led the Israelites. He protected Moses under a cleft of rock, instructing him not to even look at Him as He passed. The power of God's holiness is so strong that the people at the base of the mountain waiting for Moses to receive the Ten Commandments were warned not to touch the mountain while God was present. They would die if they did. God cannot change who He is, and He cannot come into direct contact with sin and imperfection.

There must be some kind of barrier, covering, or distance to separate that which is sinful or imperfect from His powerful presence.

Obstacle Two
(Relevant Scriptures: Deuteronomy 30:19; Joshua 24:15; Romans 11:29)

It is true that God cannot change who He is, and it is equally true that God cannot change who we are without our permission and cooperation. He made us to be free agents with a will of our own, giving us the right to make our own decisions. This is another major obstacle that stood between the reconciliation of God and His fallen citizens. This old joke says it best: "I have good news and bad news. The good news is that God gave us free will, and the bad news is that God gave us free will."

Autonomy is one of God's greatest gifts to us; without it, we would simply be programmed robots without choices of our own. Since all of God's gifts are irrevocable, our free will was something He had to deal with as He planned for our salvation. It is because of this that the plan of salvation had to include our choice to accept or reject it. The truth is God forgave humanity the moment we fell into sin. The problem for God has always been how to implement that forgiveness and get us to accept the way of salvation via our own decision.

Obstacle Three
(Relevant Scriptures: Titus 1:2; Psalms 89:34; Numbers 23:17–20; Hebrews 6:13–18)

There are other problems God faced in His efforts to find a way to reconcile Himself with humankind. These obstacles exist because of what I call God's self-imposed containment. They consist of His laws, His covenants with us, and His promises to us. He cannot lie or go against His own Word; it is simply not in His nature to do so. We can be sure that He will not change His laws that tell us what is right and what is wrong. If He makes a promise, then we can be sure that He has limited Himself to that promise. This is true for any covenant He makes with humankind. God is always faithful to His covenants, promises, and Word, even when we are not faithful to honor them.

It is because of His self-imposed containment that we can learn to trust what He says and rely on Him to do what He promises. If we think this through, then we can see how difficult it would be to trust God for our salvation if we could not count on Him to fulfill His promises and keep His covenants. Nevertheless, God's very own trustworthiness and faithfulness made it even more difficult to implement His plan to save humanity.

Obstacle Four
(Relevant Scripture: Romans 6:23)

It is because God cannot go back on His Word that salvation is also a legal matter. Not only did God have to come up with a plan of salvation, but also that plan had to answer the demands of the law in both His heavenly spiritual-realm kingdom and the naturally created realm/world here on Earth. In other words, it had to be done within the parameters of God's existing laws. This was another major issue. He had to follow the law for all involved, including Satan and his followers. The rebellion against God demanded a death sentence. The wages of sin is death, so, under the law, a price had to be paid for that sin. The challenge God faced was how to meet the demands of the law without destroying everyone who was affected by the rebellion against Him.

Summary

These are some of the issues God faced in finding a plan for the salvation of humankind. We cannot hope to understand all of the problems, but we can be sure that they were many and daunting. God had before Him the awesome task of making that which was sinful to be without sin and of making that which had become imperfect perfect again. Furthermore, He had to accomplish this without having direct contact with those who were in the state of sinfulness or imperfection. Added to these problems, the plan also had to answer the demands of the law—and it had to be each individual's choice to accept or reject it. We can see the formidable obstacles God needed to address in order to save humanity. How He designed His plan of salvation is way beyond brilliant. It takes my breath away when I think of it.

Sin is what caused imperfection, and sin is why God had to separate Himself from humankind. Nevertheless, it is God's will and desire to be reunited with all people. The entire goal of God's plan of salvation is for us to once again come into His direct presence and live in His heavenly kingdom forever. The more I learn about His magnificent plan, the more I am in awe. God, the Father designed the plan; Jesus, His Son, implemented the plan; and the Holy Spirit draws us to Christ Jesus, enabling us to accept the plan.

CHAPTER 2

THE SPIRITUAL REALM'S REBELLION

Now that we have a basic knowledge of some of the problems God faced, we need to look at the events that created the need for a plan of salvation in the first place. Traditionally, I would begin with the rebellion of Adam and Eve in the Garden of Eden, for that is where the Scriptures begin the story. However, there were actually two separate rebellions against God. The first was a spiritual-realm rebellion, and the second was the well-known rebellion of Adam and Eve. To get a more complete picture of the problems God faced, we must begin with the fall of Lucifer. It was the Lucifer-led rebellion in the spiritual realm that eventually led to Adam and Eve's rebellion in the natural realm.

The Bible tells us about Lucifer's rebellion, but the Scriptures that discuss this event appear in several different places in the Bible. The stories are given to us mainly, but not exclusively, in the books of Isaiah, Ezekiel, and Revelation. These books are prophetic in nature, dealing with spiritual-realm events that happened in the past as well as with events that are still to come. This makes it difficult to discern an exact time line of the events. The best we can do is piece together what information we have and fill in the blanks as best we can. These Scriptures include prophetic messages and symbolic visions. To have an in-depth understanding, it is helpful to study the Scriptures using reliable commentaries. This allows for different commentators' viewpoints. I list these Scriptures in parentheses after relevant chapter and section headings. I encourage you to take time to study them so that you can discern for yourself whether or not my perceptions of the ramifications of Lucifer's fall ring true.

The Fall of Lucifer/Satan
(Relevant Scriptures: Ezekiel 28:14–17; Isaiah 14:12–15; Revelation 12:3–4a; Revelation 12:7–9)

In Ezekiel 28:14–17, God describes Lucifer and his fall:

> You were anointed as a guardian cherub, for so I ordained you. You were on the holy mount of God; you walked among the fiery stones. You were blameless in your ways from the day you were created till wickedness was found in you.

> Through your widespread trade you were filled with violence, and you sinned. So I drove you from the mount of God, and I expelled you, O guardian cherub, from among the fiery stones. Your heart became proud on account of your beauty, and you corrupted your wisdom because of your splendor. So I threw you to the earth; I made a spectacle of you before kings.

This Scripture is part of a prophecy concerning the king of Tyre; however, in the above verses, God is no longer speaking to a human king but to Satan, the power behind the king of Tyre. God is speaking about the spiritual-realm cherub Lucifer who later became known as Satan. The name Lucifer means "brightness." Lucifer is the one Isaiah referred to as "O Morning Star, son of Dawn" (Isaiah 14:12). It was after Lucifer rebelled against God that his name was changed to Satan, which means "adversary," because he became the Enemy of God. It is Satan who has great power here on Earth and who is the source of the wisdom of the world system, which is in stark contrast to the wisdom of God. Throughout the history of the world, Satan has been (and still is) the source of power behind the evil rulers of this world. However, in the beginning, Lucifer was the most gifted, beautiful, and powerful of all of God's spiritual-realm citizens. He was so blessed and powerful in the spiritual realm that he became filled with pride, to the point that he considered himself greater than God. Lucifer tried to remove God from His throne and install himself instead. When he rebelled against God, he turned all the gifts and power God had bestowed on him against God and against those spiritual-realm citizens who remained loyal to God.

If we read the above Scripture carefully, we can discern that God is most likely speaking of two different events in His dealings with Lucifer. The first is when God found wickedness in Lucifer, drove him from the holy mount, and expelled him from his high position in God's kingdom. This is because anything sinful cannot survive in the presence of God. This ejection would have been sudden and violent as God drove Lucifer out of His presence. Lucifer must have run from God as far and as fast as he could until he was deep in the outer darkness of the spiritual-realm world. This was Lucifer's initial fall. The second account is when God threw Lucifer, now called Satan, to Earth. This would have occurred sometime after God created Earth and its inhabitants. There are different ways of looking at the time line, but it is safe to say that the heavens, or the spiritual-realm world, existed first and that the creation of Earth, or the natural-realm world, came at some later time.

Lucifer's rebellion was not simply a onetime event but a great war in the spiritual realm. It was the very beginning of the ongoing war between God and Satan. It is the war between good and evil that goes on to this very day in the spiritual-realm world as well as in the natural, created world here on Earth. Revelation 12:3–4(a) says, "Then another sign appeared in heaven: an enormous red dragon with seven heads and ten horns and seven crowns on his heads. His tail swept a third of the stars out of the sky and flung them to the earth." Revelation 12:7–9 says,

> And there was war in heaven. Michael [God's archangel] and his angels fought against the dragon, and the dragon and his angels fought back. But he was not strong enough, and they lost their place in heaven. The great dragon was hurled down—that ancient serpent called the devil, or Satan, who leads the whole world astray. He was hurled to the earth, and his angels with him.

The red dragon in this Scripture represents Satan. Its tail, which swept a third of the stars from the sky, stands for the angels who chose to follow Lucifer in his rebellion against God. The battles described in this Scripture, waged in the spiritual-realm world, were violent. How long they lasted we cannot know. However, I believe that they were lengthy and caused massive damage to the spiritual-realm world and its citizens. This war began when Lucifer was expelled from the mount. These initial battles of the present ongoing war between God and Satan ended with Satan and his angels being hurled to Earth.

The Repercussions of the War in the World of the Spiritual Realm

We know that when Adam and Eve rebelled against God in the Garden of Eden, it not only affected all of humankind but also affected the entire natural, created realm. It changed the peace and harmony of Earth, throwing the entire ecosystem out of balance. Similarly, it is likely that the spiritual realm was altered by Lucifer's rebellion and the war that followed. The Genesis account of what happened to the natural-realm world when Adam and Eve fell is most likely an indication of what occurred in the spiritual realm when Lucifer fell. When God was forced to expel Lucifer from the holy mount, it was the first time that God had to be separated from any of His spiritual-realm citizens. Until that moment, the entire spiritual realm had been a place of harmony and peace where all lived in the full presence of God. If I had to use only one word to describe the most important ramification of Lucifer's fall, it would be *separation*. This spiritual event made it necessary for God to separate Himself from many of His spiritual-realm citizens because they had been damaged in the great war. God's need for separation likely changed the structure of the spiritual realm, dividing it into at least three sections.

God's Heavenly Kingdom
(Relevant Scriptures: Revelation 21:21; Psalms 118:20; John 10:7)

The place we know as heaven or God's heavenly kingdom is where the full presence of God resides. It is here that we can commune fully with God and where the peace and harmony that was present before Lucifer's fall is unchanged. The only change to this section was that it was fenced off and gated. This place is exclusively for the sinless and the perfect. There are only two ways to enter through the gates of God's heavenly kingdom. We either have to be sinless and perfect—which is impossible for anyone, with the exception of Jesus, who is born into this world—or we have to accept God's plan of salvation through His Son, Jesus. It is through Jesus that we obtain His righteousness, which enables us to enter through the "pearly gates" of God's kingdom.

Hell
(Relevant Scriptures: Revelation 1:18; 2 Peter 2:4)

Until Lucifer fell, there was no need for the place known as hell. This area is the most distant from God's presence. It exists for God's enemies. Sadly, this area is also for those who have hardened their hearts to God's plan of salvation through His Son, Jesus. The people who reside here made a permanent, knowledgeable, and irrevocable decision to remain separated from the full presence of God.

Connie Becker

The Third Area of the Spiritual Realm
(Relevant Scripture: John 14:2)

Often, we acknowledge only the above two areas of the spiritual realm; however, Scripture reveals a third area that also exists in the spiritual-realm world. In the Bible are two names for this area: the bosom of Abraham and Paradise. It is my belief that *the bosom of Abraham* and *Paradise* are different names given to the third area of the spiritual realm. It is also possible that these are names for divisions within this same area. Nevertheless, the purposes of this third area are temporary, remaining only until God's plan of salvation is fully completed.

Once Lucifer rebelled, God thought it necessary to make these separations in the spiritual realm. It was not meant as a punishment, but as a protection. During our wars on Earth, there are always intended and unintended consequences of the violence. Those who participate are not the only victims of the war; even innocent people pay the price and are harmed. It is possible that the first great war in the spiritual realm was no different. Remembering that God cannot come into direct contact with sin or imperfection without destroying it, it is possible that He also had to separate Himself from some of His spiritual citizens who did not choose to follow Lucifer. It is likely that this third area was necessary for all those who were damaged by the war and could no longer live in God's full presence. It is these spiritual citizens who must make their way into this natural, created world. The third area is where they wait their turn to make the journey to Earth. This process will continue until all who need to make the journey have done so.

The Bosom of Abraham
(Relevant Scriptures: Luke 16:19–31; Luke 23:43; 2 Corinthians 12:2–4; Ephesians 4:8; 1 Peter 3:18–22)

The bosom of Abraham, also referred to as Abraham's side, is located within the third area of the spiritual realm. It is a place meant for what some call the righteous dead. Abraham was a man of faith. He believed God but would not have had the opportunity to accept Christ because Jesus had not yet provided the way of salvation. The gate to God's heavenly kingdom was not open to anyone who had come to Earth until after the resurrection of Christ Jesus. The bosom of Abraham is where the people of faith and the seekers of God who died before Jesus died and was resurrected resided. They waited there until Jesus opened the way for them to enter through the gates of heaven.

The word *bosom* is a perfect description of the purpose of the third area of the spiritual realm. *Protection, harbor, encompass,* and *embrace* are some words that pertain to the bosom. The bosom is the front area of the body between the arms. At the center of the bosom is the heart. The arms can enfold across the bosom, creating an area of holding. This gives us a heartwarming picture of this third area of the spiritual realm, which is just that, a holding place. It is where the people of faith who died before Jesus was resurrected waited for Him to come and lead them into God's gated heavenly kingdom.

Paradise

As Jesus died on the cross, He told the man who was being crucified next to Him, "Today you will be with me in Paradise."(Luke 23:43) He couldn't have been speaking about the gated area of the spiritual realm, because He did not go to that area immediately. Instead, He went into the area where all of those spirits who lived on Earth and died before His resurrection were waiting for Him. He then preached to them, giving them the opportunity to accept Him or reject Him. At some point, He led all those who accepted His salvation into the gated area we call heaven. Because of this, I believe that the bosom of Abraham and Paradise are both located in the third area of the spiritual realm.

Purgatory

The Roman Catholic Church teaches about a spiritual-realm area called purgatory. If I understand the teaching correctly, this is an area where the process of sanctification is completed in some individuals after they die. Sanctification is the process that believers go through after they have accepted Jesus as their Savior to become perfect in Christ. The Catholic Church teaches that this process continues for some individuals after they die. It is the Catholic belief that some individuals need further cleansing and purifying before they can enter the gated area of the spiritual realm. This is another possible example of the existence of a third area of the spiritual realm that is neither heaven nor hell.

I have some reservations about this teaching because I believe we are saved by the righteousness of Christ alone, so there is no other sacrifice needed for us to enter into God's full presence. My understanding is that for all who have accepted Christ as their Savior, these things are accomplished within the gates of God's heavenly kingdom and under the covering of the righteousness of Christ.

I imagine that the gated area of the spiritual realm is similar to a large American city. The city is surrounded by the countryside, then the suburbs, then the city limits, and, finally, the heart of the city, which is the throne of God. As Christians, we all live in God's presence; however, we may start our life in God's heavenly kingdom in different parts of the city. It's all good and all wonderful, and we can continue to grow from wherever we start. Jesus used the example of a house to explain the divisions in the gated area of the spiritual realm. He told his disciples, "In my Father's house there are many rooms; if it were not so, I would have told you. I am going there to prepare a place for you" (John 14:2).

Possible Current Uses for the Third Area
(Relevant Scripture: John 20:10–18)

There are some who believe that this third area is no longer active and was closed after Jesus preached to the people who died before His resurrection and after He led those who accepted Him into the gated area of heaven. One belief is that this section of the spiritual realm had served its purpose and was permanently closed. I cannot accept this. To me, it does not make sense and leaves me with questions that would otherwise have answers. I believe it is possible that this area is still active and God now uses it for several different purposes.

I do believe there is something significant about the time lapse between Jesus' death and the resurrection of His body. He died on Friday and was raised on Sunday. When Mary Magdalene found Jesus alive at the gravesite, she wanted to touch Him, but He stopped her, saying, "Do not hold on to me for I have not yet returned to the Father" (John 20:17). He was still in some kind of transition. We know that He was spiritually active in the third area of the spiritual realm during this time, yet He had not personally returned to the Father. I believe it is possible that we will all go through a process of transition at the time of our death. This process most likely takes place in the third area of the spiritual realm, before we enter the gates of heaven.

Summary

We cannot claim to understand all the conditions and principles of the spiritual realm or how it works. In addition, I do not grasp why God did not simply destroy Lucifer and his angels during the initial battles of the war. I suspect that it was a legal matter in the spiritual realm that God had to honor. Most likely, it involves the power and position God had given to Lucifer. I do not doubt that there was enormous damage inflicted on many spiritual-realm citizens and that God was forced to separate Himself from them. Nevertheless, I cannot say for sure what damage was done to them. My personal belief is that a seed of confusion and doubt about God took root in their spirits. No matter the exact consequences for His spiritual citizens, God was left to deal with tragic and enormous spiritual-realm problems.

Even though the time line of these spiritual-realm events causes some confusion, one thing is certain: God expelled Satan from His heavenly kingdom and hurled him to Earth. Earth is the place God chose for fighting His final battles with Satan. Earth is also where He gives us, His spiritual-realm citizens, the opportunity to choose for ourselves whom we will believe and whom we will follow. It is my belief that the natural, created world is being used to cleanse and restore the spiritual-realm world so that we may return to it and live once again in complete harmony and in the full presence of God.

CHAPTER 3

THE ULTIMATE PURPOSE OF THE NATURAL-REALM WORLD

(Relevant Scriptures: 1 John 4:16; Psalms 106:44–45, 117:2; Exodus 2:24–25; Hosea 11:1–9)

The opening line of the Holy Bible declares, "In the beginning God created the heavens and the earth."(Genesis 1:1) However, the question that nagged me off and on for years is, why? Why did He create Earth and why did He create us? One commonly given reason is that God is the Creator, so He is always creating. We are simply part of His creative work. The most common explanation is that God is love, so He created a people to love and who, in turn, could love and worship Him. While these explanations are part of the truth, I do not believe that they are the main reason why God created us. God is foreknowing. He did not create this world and afterward become surprised when humankind fell into sin, leaving Him with a massive problem to solve. So, the question remained: Why did He create us?

The creation story is among my favorites. But I remember the questions that would pop into my mind when I was a child as I learned those precious verses. Why did God give us free will and then place the Tree of the Knowledge of Good and Evil right in the center of the Garden of Eden? Why did God allow Satan into the garden, thereby giving him access to Adam and Eve? If Adam and Eve were good, then why did they knowingly disobey God? From time to time over the years, these nagging questions would come to the forefront of my mind as I advanced my efforts to know God.

As I grasped the truth that God is love and that love, by its very nature, makes one vulnerable to the objects of love, I understood that the pain and suffering this world inflicts upon God's created children is costly, not only to us, but also to God, who experiences great anguish as a result. So, I added the following questions to my growing list: Why did He allow this world to go on? Why not make some kind of provision for the people He had already created and then destroy this world, ending the pain and suffering? Scripture clearly reveals that a day will come when this world as we know it will have served its purpose. What determines the timing of the end of the world has tantalized the minds of many theologians over the centuries. It is as if there are certain natural-realm events that must take place, or perhaps a predetermined number of souls who must be born, before God will put an end to this sinful world.

These questions, along with my growing trust in the Lord, helped me to realize that there had to be something very important to God and for us, His created children, for Him to put Himself and us through the suffering that is part of life in this world. Given this, I added two more questions to my list: (1) What is so very important to God that He would allow His creation to go through the suffering that this world inflicts? (2) What is the ultimate purpose of this world?

Revelations
(Relevant Scripture: Ephesians 1:4–10)

A revelation, at least for me, most often starts with a kernel of knowledge that grows into a deeper understanding. It is like a living puzzle. Each revelation adds something to my understanding until, finally, the pieces start to fall into place and I can see the whole picture. The above questions represent a spiritual puzzle that the Holy Spirit put together for me over the course of many years. Sometimes, I would receive tiny pieces of this giant puzzle, but they were small and never quite fit together. Then one day, I had a revelation that was a much larger piece of the puzzle. It was that God did not first create Earth and its inhabitants only for them to become a huge problem. Instead, He created this natural-realm world to solve an already existing spiritual-realm problem. The possibility that He created this world to solve the problems of the spiritual world became even more real to me with the astonishing revelation that the human body was the first covering for sin. It was almost magical how everything started to make sense to me. My long-held questions started to be answered.

God's Magnificent Plan
(Relevant Scriptures: Romans 8:29–30; 1 Peter 1:20–21)

It was in the spiritual realm that God was first faced with the need for a plan of salvation and reconciliation with some of His spiritual-realm citizens. A plan is a diagram or a blueprint that maps out the steps and methods to be followed to achieve a purpose. A plan predetermines the course of action to be followed, whether it is constructing a building or solving an existing problem. It was in the spiritual-realm world that God, the Father designed His magnificent plan of salvation long before He created this natural-realm world called Earth. He specifically designed the plan to deal with the problem of all of the spiritual realm's citizens that had been damaged in the wake of Lucifer's fall and could no longer come into His direct presence. These spiritual citizens were not necessarily enemies of God. They were victims in a terrible spiritual-realm happening.

The apostle Paul wrote of God's predetermined plan in Romans 8:29–30, which reads, "For those God foreknew he also predestined to be conformed to the likeness of his Son, that he might be the firstborn among many brothers. And those he predestined, he also called; those he called, he also justified; those he justified, he also glorified." The meaning of this scripture can be a source of misunderstanding. At first glance, it seems to say that there are those of us who are predestined to accept Jesus, even though it is clear that we need to make our own choice about Him. However, if you read this scripture knowing that Paul is speaking about God's plan of salvation for His spiritual-realm citizens, then it takes on an entirely different meaning. It becomes easier to discern what Paul is actually saying. Let's look at these verses one line at a time to get a clearer understanding of what they are saying.

For those God foreknew he also predestined to be conformed to the likeness of his Son that he might be the firstborn among many brothers.

Who are those whom Paul says that "God foreknew"? They are all the spiritual-realm citizens affected by Lucifer's fall. They are the ones who could no longer enter into God's direct presence because of the harm done to them by the spiritual realm war. God foreknows them because they are His spiritual-realm citizens who existed before the creation of this world.

It is not such a stretch to believe that we existed in the spiritual realm before this world was created. We know that inside every living human being is a yearning to find God. This is because the personal spirit, deep within, remembers God and the spiritual-realm world where it once lived. The spirit is constantly searching to find God and commune with Him once more. This Scripture informs us that God knew us before we were born because we existed first in the spiritual realm. It is all these spiritual realm citizens who, through God's plan to save and reunite with them, were predestined to be born into this natural-realm world with a mission of seeking their own redemption.

The reason they were born into this natural-realm world was to be "conformed to the likeness of his Son," who is Jesus. The first thing this tells us is that, through God's predetermined plan, Jesus was predestined, before the foundation of this world was laid, to be the Savior of humankind. Jesus was predestined to be the Way back into the full presence of God for all of those spiritual-realm citizens. What is "the likeness of His Son"? Jesus is true God and true Man. In Him, the reunion of God and humankind was first accomplished. Through Him, the reunion of our individual spirits with God's Spirit is made possible. This means that when we accept Jesus, God's predetermined plan of salvation, we are conformed to the likeness of Jesus, His Son, and reunited with God's Spirit.

And those he predestined, he also called; those he called, he also justified; those he justified, he also glorified.

God's foreknowledge of these spiritual-realm citizens goes deeper than His simply knowing each individual. He also knows who among them is going to accept and reject His plan of salvation. This does not mean that God predestined some of His spiritual-realm citizens to accept His plan of salvation; it simply means that God knows beforehand who will and who will not accept Jesus as Savior.

I like to use the analogy of a weather forecaster to help provide a better perspective of God's foreknowledge. The weather is predicted by a person who has foreknowledge of the weather patterns and how they will likely manifest in the future. The weather forecaster does not cause the conditions of the weather; he or she only foreknows the conditions that determine the weather. A weather forecaster's knowledge is imperfect. He or she can only predict the weather—with varying degrees of success. God's foreknowledge is perfect. He knows in advance those who will and those who will not accept His plan of salvation.

Every citizen of the spiritual realm whom God predestined to come to Earth is called by God and given an opportunity to accept Jesus as Savior, but not all of them are going to accept Him. To answer the demands of the law, God gives all souls the opportunity to make the decision to accept or reject His Way of salvation. No one is predestined by God, apart from their own decision, to accept Jesus as the Savior. Every individual spirit has the free will to make its own decision. God, through His plan of salvation, simply provides the Way and makes conditions right for people to be reunited with Him, if they so desire.

Even though all are called to accept God's predetermined plan of salvation, there are those who have specific callings on their lives as they live on Earth. These individual callings are determined by God's foreknowledge of each spiritual-realm citizen. In other words, some are called because God knows they will be people of faith, and some are called to certain positions because God foreknows that they will never come to Him. God can use those who accept his plan and also those who reject it to help Him implement His predetermined plan of salvation.

The story of Pharaoh is an example of God using an individual who resisted His will to release the Jewish nation out of bondage and slavery. Time after time, Pharaoh resisted God until God hardened his heart. However, Pharaoh would never have been put in this position if God had not foreknown that he would never come to God for his salvation. Abraham is an example of a man of faith that God called to receive His everlasting covenant of salvation through faith. Abraham was in this position because God foreknew that he would believe Him and be a person of faith, eventually accepting God's predetermined plan of salvation.

It is God's sovereign choice to have mercy on whom He decides and to harden whom He wants to harden. To understand this, we must first know that God makes these decisions out of His perfect foreknowledge of each individual spiritual-realm citizen. God neither makes mistakes in this nor makes choices based on favoritism. God knows who will and will not accept Him as the Savior. I know in the deepest part of my soul that not one individual who would ever accept Jesus as his or her Savior will be forever lost and separated from God.

Called, Justified, Glorified

Paul then writes about the order of salvation. We are spiritual-realm citizens called to be born into this world and carry out a mission of our own redemption and healing. This is preordained. All who accept God's plan of salvation through the life, death, and resurrection of Jesus are justified in Christ. Those who are justified in Christ are also predestined to be glorified and return to the spiritual-realm world to spend all eternity in God's heavenly kingdom, living in the full presence of God. This is God's magnificent plan for the salvation of humankind. The plan was predetermined in the spiritual-realm world before the foundation of this natural realm world was created.

Connie Becker

Answers

Why Did God Create This Natural-Realm World?
(Relevant Scriptures: Revelation 21:1–5; 2 Corinthians 5:17–19)

Revelation 21:1–4 says,

> Then I saw a new heaven and a new earth, for the first heaven and the first earth had passed away, and there was no longer any sea. I saw the Holy City, the New Jerusalem, coming down out of heaven from God, prepared as a bride beautifully dressed for her husband. And I heard a loud voice from the throne saying, "Now the dwelling of God is with men, and he will live with them. They will be his people, and God himself will be with them and be their God. He will wipe every tear from their eyes. There will be no more death or mourning or crying or pain, for the old order of things has passed away."

This is a picture of the fulfillment of God's ultimate purpose for creating this natural-realm world. God's goal is to carry out His plan of salvation by reuniting His Spirit with our individual spirits. In this vision, the apostle John saw both a new heaven and a new earth. This indicates that the spiritual-realm world, like the natural-realm world, was completely cleansed of and healed from the damage done to it. In this vision, God is able to be fully present and reside with all His spiritual-realm citizens, including those who had come to Earth and accepted Jesus as their Savior.

For a number of reasons, God chose to handle the spiritual realm's problems by creating this natural-realm world. One of those reasons was a matter of containment. For one thing, the spiritual realm is eternal; there is no passing of time there. This enables the separation of God and His spiritual citizens to go on forever. So, He created a place subject to the passing of time and, in so doing, limited the amount of time for sin and separation to exist. In addition, God contained our individual spirits in bodies of flesh. In so doing, He provided a temporary covering between Himself and our damaged spirits so that He could interact more closely with us. He was unable to be in close contact with His damaged citizens in the spiritual realm because there was no covering between Him and them. He solved this problem by creating a place of solid form and matter, which enabled Him to have a closer interaction with His people. There are other reasons why this natural-realm world is critical to God's plan of salvation. I reveal these reasons in more detail in the chapters that follow.

This world as we know it will one day come to an end. Until that time, we are working through the problems that began in the spiritual realm. I believe that there are certain natural-realm events that must take place and a set number of spirits that must be born into this world before God will put an end to this sinful world. During the time spent on

Earth, each individual has decisions to make, as there are battles to be won in the war between good and evil.

Why Did God Allow Satan Access to Adam and Eve?

Why did God give us free will and then place the Tree of the Knowledge of Good and Evil right in the center of the Garden of Eden? And why did God allow Satan into the garden, thereby giving him access to Adam and Eve? I discovered that these two questions actually have the same answer. It is simply a matter of choice.

First, there is no free will without choice. The two circumstances—the existence of the tree and the presence of Satan—provided Adam and Eve with a clear choice: follow God's wishes or follow Satan's wishes. God instructed them not to eat the fruit from the Tree of the Knowledge of Good and Evil and clearly told them that they would die if they did. Satan was allowed into the garden so he could present his will to Adam and Eve. They were given a clear choice of whom to believe and whom to follow. God was honoring His gift of free will. At the same time, He was fulfilling a requirement of a spiritual-realm law.

If Adam and Eve Were Perfect, Then Why Did They Disobey God?

I've basically answered this question. Whatever effect Lucifer's fall had on God's spiritual citizens, it altered them in some way. I suspect that a seed of rebellion against or some doubt about God was planted in their spirits, so when the spirits of Adam and Eve were placed in their bodies, whatever damage had been done was there with them. When God looked at them and said that what He had created was good, He was speaking of their bodies. It did not mean that the spirits within them were perfect. Their spirits were already flawed—and that is the reason why they were in a body in the first place.

Why Does God Allow Suffering?
(Scripture Relevant: 1Timothy 2:3–5)

A question that bothers many is: Why does God allow suffering to go on? Suffering touches all of us, Christians and non-Christians, equally. It affects the good and the bad alike. We often view it as a punishment, asking ourselves, *What did I do wrong to deserve this suffering?* Yet, we watch the innocent of this world suffer untold misery they can't possibly deserve. So, the question haunts us: Why does a loving God allow suffering to continue?

The question has never been about whether or not God was going to allow suffering, because suffering became a fact when sin came into being. The issue was how God would deal with the suffering and for how long he would permit any one individual to suffer. As previously stated, the creation of the natural-realm world actually limits the amount of time the suffering can continue. We must first understand that sin and suffering were never something God wanted us to experience. However, once sin became part of our existence, He had to deal with it. God designed the plan of salvation in the way He did because it is the only way to accomplish the salvation of humankind. Once the rebellion in the spiritual realm took place, He was left with the problems created by it. He allows this world to go on so, eventually, the spiritual realm and the natural realm can come together, free of sin and the suffering it causes.

The truth is, you cannot stop suffering until the cause of the suffering is eliminated. Suffering is caused by our separation from God and the sin that causes that separation. Many things God does are aimed to destroy the sin that causes suffering. One day, sin will be completely defeated. If He were to destroy the suffering now, then He would have to put an end to this world. If this world were destroyed prematurely, then any spirit that had not yet journeyed to this created-realm world would be lost and separated from God for all eternity. These souls would never be able to make the choice to accept God's plan of salvation. They would live for all eternity separated from the full presence of God, unable to enter His heavenly kingdom. God's will is that none shall perish, so He allows the suffering to continue for a limited amount of time until all affected individuals have the chance to accept or reject His plan of salvation.

None of us will know in advance the exact moment when this world will end. However, there will be no need for this world when every soul that would accept God's plan for salvation has done so. This is what determines when God will put an end to the world as we know it. God's ultimate purpose for this world is the eternal salvation of our spirits and souls. He wants us to be with Him. The thought of losing even one soul that would have accepted Christ is unthinkable. This is what is so very important to God. It is also the reason why He allows this world, with all its heartache and suffering, to continue.

God Helps Us in Our Suffering

There are many things that God does to help us in our suffering. When God gave us the Ten Commandments, he revealed the principles we may follow to help us avoid many pitfalls that can cause suffering for ourselves and others. We often think of the Ten Commandments as a list of rules God wants us to follow in order to please Him. We do not realize that He gave us those rules so we could avoid the inevitable consequences of breaking them. In other words, the consequences of breaking the Ten Commandments were in place long before He gave us His law. By giving us those commandments, He revealed how to avoid some of the consequences of sin. Doing our best to follow God's ways and instructions will not save us from all suffering, but living His way to the best of our ability will certainly save us from performing many actions that cause our suffering.

There are other ways God helps us avoid suffering. He teaches us natural-realm principles about how to care for our bodies, helping us to avoid sickness and suffering. He teaches scientists, doctors, psychiatrists, pastors, and others many ways to care for and heal our bodies, minds, and spirits so that our suffering is limited. Although we sometimes forget to think of it in this way, death puts an end to our suffering in this world, allowing our spirits to go back to the spiritual-realm world. We must remember that God suffers with us and will always give us the strength and grace to endure whatever befalls us.

CHAPTER 4

CREATION: PART ONE OF GOD'S PLAN OF SALVATION

(Relevant Scriptures: Genesis 1–2:3; Psalms 104; Romans 1:20; Hebrews 11:3)

The Old Testament is the written record of the first phase of God's plan for salvation. The story begins with, "In the beginning God created the heavens and the earth."(Genesis 1:1) In these few simple words, God declares that He is the Creator of this natural-realm world and the heavens surrounding it. Next, He begins the process of solving the problems of the spiritual realm by creating this natural-realm world we call Earth.

The process of creation is described with these words: "Now the earth was formless and empty, darkness was over the surface of the deep, and the Spirit of God was hovering over the waters" (Genesis 1:2). The picture that comes to my mind is one of great power and motion hovering over the water as God prepares to bring forth life, thus beginning the first phase of salvation. It is the same picture I have of the Holy Spirit as God begins the second phase of the plan of salvation. The same power that was present at the time of creation hovered over the Virgin Mary as He prepared for the birth of His sinless Son.

"Then God said, 'Let there be light,' and there was light." (Genesis 1:3) Then, He separated the light from the darkness, creating day and night. It appears simple enough until you start to think about that word *light*. *The Grosset WebsterDictionary* defines light as "a wave motion of radiant energy which renders the environment visible." It was at that moment that God began to make that which was invisible visible. All creation confirms the existence of God, thus making the invisible God visible. He also patterned this created world after the spiritual-realm world; thus, the invisible spiritual realm became visible. If you are curious about what God's heavenly kingdom is like, just look around, for you are living in a place fashioned in the likeness of His kingdom.

The second day, God said, "Let there be an expanse between the waters to separate water from water." God called the expanse "sky." (Genesis 1:6, 8) I find it fascinating that God put a dome around this world and then divided the waters and the dome, keeps that life-giving water in our atmosphere. The same water is recycled and cleaned, made new over and over again. Jesus uses creation to describe what He is to us when He tells the woman at the well that He is living water and those who drink it will thirst no more. Once we accept Jesus, we have life-giving energy constantly flowing through our soul and spirit. This energy refreshes and cleanses us over and over again.

Next, God commanded the waters to gather in one place and let the dry land appear. After this, all conditions were right for vegetation to begin growing. God said, "Let the earth put forth vegetation, plants yielding seed and trees bearing fruit in which is their seed, each according to its own kind" (Genesis 1:12). God put all of the plants in a place where conditions were right for them to grow so they would produce what was necessary for what He created next.

The fourth day of creation is intriguing to me because God takes His larger creation, light, and encloses it in luminaries in the sky. For the daytime, we have the stronger light, the sun, and for the nighttime, we have the softer lights of the moon and stars. As we remember the definition of light as "a wave motion of radiant energy," it would seem that when God enclosed this motion in the sun and moon, time and the seasons became a reality. This motion controls the oceans' tides and tells the birds when to migrate, the fish when to spawn, and the leaves when to bud and when to fall.

The fifth day brought the creation of the birds and the fishes. God blessed them by saying, "Be fruitful and increase in number."(Genesis 1:22) The sixth day was the day when

He created animals and human beings. When reading the Scriptures about the sixth day, I have the impression that the day was divided. First, God said, "Let the land produce living creatures according to their kinds."(Genesis 1:24) Just as God commanded, it was so, and God looked and saw that it was good. Then, God turned to creating His crowning glory, humankind. Everything He had created up to this point was to make conditions right and have a place for this, His most magnificent creation. Psalms 139:14 declares, "I praise you because I am fearfully and wonderfully made." The Earth and all its inhabitants are just that, fearfully and wonderfully made, especially humankind, for people are created in the very image of God.

CHAPTER 5

CREATED IN THE IMAGE OF GOD

(Relevant Scriptures: Genesis 1:26–27; Hebrews 4:12; 1 Thessalonians 5:23–24; Psalms 139:14)

God began the human race by creating Adam and Eve, declaring them to be created in His own image. The triune God made us in three separate parts: a spirit and a soul housed in a body, all functioning as one unit. He created a person to be an independent, reasoning, free moral agent with the ability to choose and the intelligence to rule over all creation. He gave us personalities and talents. God's own creativity flows through us. He bestowed upon us a full range of emotions along with the capacity to love and worship. Is it any wonder that through the ages, humankind has struggled with the false assumption that we are our own god?

To grow in our understanding of God, we must establish a relationship with the Father, the Son, and the Holy Spirit.

To have a clearer awareness of ourselves, we have to identify with our body, our soul, and our spirit. If we desire to have a deeper comprehension of how God's plan of salvation works, then we first need to understand the three parts of our being and how they function together. This is because God designed us for the ultimate purpose of saving our spirits and souls. In other words, we are literally designed to be saved.

The Body
(Relevant Scriptures: Genesis 2:7, 21–22; 2 Peter 1:13–14; 2 Corinthians 5:1; Luke 2:1–20)

The human body is a remarkable creation. I do not understand the intricacies of how it is put together and the wonderful way in which it works. It is amazing to me that something so complex was formed largely of water and dust from the ground: water and dirt, the two elements spoken of as God began His creative work. Our bodies were formed from the dust of the ground and to dust they will return. The human body is part of this natural-realm world, which is left behind when our spirits and souls return to the spiritual-realm world. In other words, the spirit and soul are eternal, while the human body is temporal.

The earthly body is basically the house or, as the apostle Paul calls it, the tent we live in. A tent is a temporary, movable dwelling place. Likewise, the body houses the soul and the spirit, allowing us to move freely from place to place. While the body has its needs and duties to perform, for the most part it is led and controlled by the soul and the spirit. Nevertheless, one of the main purposes of the body is to provide a covering or barrier for the soul and the spirit so we may interact more closely with God.

The human body also provides the covering necessary for the fullness of God to enter into the atmosphere of this created world in a completely new way. It was into a human body that Jesus, the Son of God, was incarnated, enabling Him to become one with humankind. When reading the story of the night when Christ Jesus was born, I pictured it almost like a children's Christmas Eve program. Baby Jesus was in the manger, the shepherds were in the fields, and the bright shining star was in the sky. All was quiet. I imagine it much differently now. I believe the power released into this world at the moment of Christ's birth charged the universe and caused a great and magnificent star to form. The star of Bethlehem was such a phenomenon that even faraway astronomers observed it and knew that an extraordinary birth had occurred. The spiritual realm was aware of the event, too. A host of angels could be seen as the shepherds watched their flocks. That night, the fullness of God took on the flesh of humanity and manifested as a tiny newborn body wrapped in swaddling clothes and humbly lying in a manger. It is characteristic of God to stage a cosmic event in a humble setting. Never has He done it better than at the birth of His only begotten Son.

The Human Spirit
(Relevant Scriptures: Numbers 27:15–16; Luke 1:47, 8:53–55; Galatians 6:18; Acts 7:59; Ecclesiastes 12:7)

The spirit area is the most mysterious of the three parts, for it houses the very essence of who we are as individuals. Our human spirit is of the spiritual-realm world and is eternal, making it harder for us in the created-realm world to understand. As I shared before, I believe that the individual human spirit had a life in the spiritual realm long before this created world existed and that it comes into this world with a past and history all its own. Whether you agree with this theory or you believe that each new baby born has a newly created spirit, one fact is the same: Each individual spirit is so valuable to God that He goes to great lengths to protect it, save it from harm, and redeem it for all eternity.

Our spirit and our soul are in separate areas, but they work so closely together that it makes it difficult to discern how they are divided. What makes the most sense to me is that each individual spirit has its own unique personality, a continuous supply of God's very own creativity, and the awesome ability to know God intimately.

The Human Personality
(Relevant Scripture: Romans 12:1–8)

A popular thought some years ago was that a newborn baby was like a blank canvas and its environment alone would determine what the child would become. While it is certainly true that the love, nurturing, training, and teaching, or sadly sometimes the lack of these things plays an important part in determining the growth of each individual, it is equally evident that a baby is not a blank canvas. It does not take new parents long to discover that they are dealing with a little one who, right from the start, has his or her own temperament. When my identical-twin grandsons were small, it was difficult for most people to tell them apart, but once you knew their personalities, it was easy to determine who was who in that sweet duo. They may have looked alike, but each little body housed a completely different spirit with a personality all its own.

Our human spirit is the very essence of who we are, and our personality is the core of our spirit area. Although the personality will be influenced and matured by the environment and its interaction with the soul, it will remain basically the same throughout our life on Earth and into eternity. Our personality is to our spirit what DNA is to our body. It is each individual's basic pattern. Just as the body follows the specific pattern of its DNA, the human spirit follows its own unique makeup. Our choices, situations, and psyche can affect our body and our personality but cannot change the basic pattern.

In Paul's letter to the Romans, he lists seven gifts. These gifts are the seven basic personality types. They are sometimes referred to as motivational gifts because they determine how we see the world and supply the basic motivation for all that we do. These gifts are also referred to as spiritual gifts because they are part of the human spirit and are possessed by all of God's created children. Each personality type has its own set of characteristics, both positive and negative. Our individual personalities are made up of all seven personality types, with one or two being dominant. It is the dominant personalities that determine the basic strengths and weaknesses of our personality.

It is to everyone's advantage to learn the traits of their own personality type. The ultimate purpose of knowing our personality is so we can discern God's will for us. Our personality makeup is one of the indicators we can use to find our place in His created world and especially in the body of Christ when we become Christians. For a long time, the secular world has known the benefits of personality types. Colleges and employers alike give tests to discover the types in an effort to lead and place people where they will be the happiest, the most fulfilled, and the most efficient.

I have always found it interesting that there are seven personality types. The number seven is often said to be God's perfect number. I suspect that if we could discern what the personality would be like if all seven types were present in perfect balance, then we would know the personality of Jesus. Our personality is just one more thing that shows how God created us in His own image.

God's Creative Flow
(Relevant Scriptures: Ephesians 2:10; Isaiah 54:16; Matthew 25:14–30)

Another way in which God's image is reflected in humanity is through God's own creativity flowing through the human spirit. Humankind was created with the ability to follow dreams and realize them through God's creative flow. Whenever individual creativity is stifled, whether in a government, a business, an organization, or an individual, you can expect to find diminished success and decline. On the other hand, if this gift is nurtured and given the freedom to grow, then it is inexhaustible and progressive. It is through this gift that we actually become partners with God, the great Creator, in His work of creativity.

During a drive through downtown Indianapolis, I received a revelation about this very subject. There is something about beautiful buildings set in just the right surroundings that thrills me. I was admiring the beautiful architecture when I suddenly stopped myself, fearing that I was on the verge of worshiping human-made structures. I said a silent prayer: "Lord, these buildings are so beautiful." At that moment, the Holy Spirit broke into my thoughts. He revealed to me that when I look at nature, it is the creative work He alone has done, but when I look at the buildings, it is the creative work He has done in partnership with humankind. This has changed how I look at things. I now see God more clearly working through all of His created children. It is amazing to see what we can accomplish when we allow His creative flow to operate through us.

Creativity reaches into all areas of life and is part of everything we do. The artist, the musician, the chef, the teacher, the doctor, the scientist, the photographer, the seamstress, the designer, the homemaker, the builder, the crafter, the mechanic, the farmer, the dancer, the plumber, the carpenter ... all of us are in partnership with the great Creator. Every work of art, beautiful structure, piece of lovely music, poem or other literary work, well-designed piece of clothing, delicious recipe, well-appointed garden, invention, scientific finding, and much more all had its beginning in God's creative flow.

The spirit area functions together with the soul. When our creativity is blended with our knowledge, desires, and hard work, then our talents develop. We are all born with the gift of God's creative flow; however, He does not give the gift in equal measure. Some are given many talents and are conscious of this flow right from the start. Others have to search out their talents and may begin with only one. This seems unfair until you understand the secret of God's creative flow and the development process of talents. Talent produces more talent. No matter what measure of talent you have been given, if you take it, use it, and keep moving forward, then that one talent will turn to two and so on, until you can easily surpass the person who was initially given more talents. It is the very nature of God's creative flow to increase according to demand. Scripture informs us that when we enter into God's creativity, we enter into His happiness, for God, at His heart, is a Creator, an artist, and a worker.

One thing that makes our personality and talents so special is that we possess them as gifts. When we make Jesus the Lord of our life, we can offer these gifts for His use to further His kingdom. This makes our bodies a living sacrifice for spiritual worship, as these are the gifts housed in the human spirit.

The Ability to Know God
(Relevant Scripture: Hosea 6:6 Living Bible; Romans 8:16, 1Corinthians 6:17; John 4:24, 14: 6, 15-21, 26)

Tucked away in one of the smaller books of the Bible is a verse that is among my favorites. I found it one night when I randomly opened *The Living Bible* to the book of Hosea. God is speaking and says, "I don't want your sacrifices—I want your love; I don't want your offerings—I want you to know me." Those words seemed to jump off the page at me and change my heart forever. It was as if majestic God was humbly telling me that He wanted me to know Him and love

Him. I believe that God's ultimate will and deepest desire is that all of us come to know Him and love Him. In return, He gives us His all-encompassing love. Love is what motivates God to do everything He does for His created children.

Few things are more painful than being separated from those we love. When our individual spirit and God's Spirit were forced to separate, it caused a deep longing in both spirits to be together again. The Holy Spirit is constantly seeking and wooing us to accept Jesus as our Savior so He can reunite with our human spirit. God has done, and continues to do, everything in His power to make that reunion possible for all of us. Likewise, the human spirit is restlessly searching to be reunited with God's Spirit and will not be completely at rest until this reunion is accomplished. It is in our spirit area that this reunion must take place.

It is only with the spirit that we can intimately know God. If we know Him only with our intellect, then we merely know about Him. Intellectual knowledge alone is insufficient to truly know or worship Him. It is a fact that you cannot love what you do not know and you cannot worship what you do not love. It is written in John 4:24 that "God is spirit, and his worshipers must worship him in spirit and in truth." We cannot truly worship God until our spirit is united with Him. Our spirit cannot be reunited with God's Spirit until we accept the truth. Jesus describes Himself as the truth. He also explained to His disciples that no one comes to the Father except through the Son, and no one receives the Holy Spirit except through Jesus.

He is the truth that opens the only way for our spirit and God's Spirit to be reunited. He is also the only way we can return to God the Father and live in His full presence in His heavenly kingdom.

There is only one way for the human spirit to be reunited with God's Holy Spirit. It must be born again of the Spirit of God. The need to be born again suggests that something was once alive and is now dead. It is shocking to realize that when we are born into this world, we are actually spiritually dead to God. The definition of the word *death* involves separation. This does not mean that the individual spirit is dead. It means that we are separated from God's Spirit.

The Soul

The Greek word for *soul* is *psyche,* which refers to our psychological makeup. The soul is the vital part of us that allows us to function as free agents. The soul consists of the mind, the will, and the emotions. It is where we find our intellect, desires, drives, and feelings. The deepest part of the soul houses what is known as the "heart of man." What an amazing part of our created being is the soul with its ability to take in information and not only comprehend its meaning but also store it in the memory. This entire process allows us to learn and evaluate the information and then make decisions accordingly. In addition, the soul is where we have the God-given ability to experience love. In order to gain deeper understanding of the salvation of the soul, we need a basic understanding of what goes on in its different areas.

The Mind
(Relevant Scriptures Psalms 26:2; 1Corinthians 2:9; Luke10:27; Jeremiah 17:10; Romans 12:2; Galatians 5:16-18

The human mind consists of two major parts: the conscious and the subconscious. The conscious mind is a very busy place that houses the intellect. It is where all the different influences that come into our lives are first processed. Our minds are constantly taking in and processing information gathered from our senses of sight, hearing, taste, touch, and smell. One would think that this would be enough for the conscious mind to do, but, unfortunately, this part of our mind is also a battleground. This is so because who or what controls the deepest part of the mind can influence our entire being.

The Wars of the Mind
(Relevant Scriptures: 2Corinthians 2:9-11; Ephesians 6:12; 1Corinthians 10:13; James 1:13; Galatians 5:16-18)

Two major wars take place in the mind. The first war, known as the war between good and evil, is between God and Satan. Satan does his best to influence us to follow him.

He tempts us by offering what appeals to the sinful nature, trying to subject us to pitfalls. His goal is to keep us from knowing God and following God's ways. God, on the other hand, is constantly trying to encourage us to live godly lives and to protect us as much as possible from the consequences of sin. At the same time, He is doing everything in His power to lead us to His Son, so we can be reunited with the Holy Spirit, thereby enabling us to spend eternity in His loving presence. At times, it truly does feel as if we have a little devil on one shoulder and a little angel on the other, each trying to influence us. The truth is that, because of our free will, neither God nor Satan can make us do anything. We decide what to do by using the information processed in the mind.

The second war that takes place in the conscious mind is a war against one's self. This war takes place between our soul area and our spirit area and is often called the war between the flesh and the spirit. This war begins, or at least increases, once we have accepted Christ as our Savior and have been born again of the Spirit of God. Our spirit area was designed to rule over the area of our soul; however, when the Spirit of God was forced to leave the human soul, the human spirit was not strong enough on its own to control the soul. So, when we are born again of God's Spirit, our spirit area rises up to take its rightful place as leader of the soul. Since the soul is accustomed to calling the shots, it rebels and the battle begins. While this war begins in the spirit area and in the subconscious mind, it spills over into the conscious mind.

Deep Mind

(Relevant Scriptures: Matthew 15:11, 17-20; Genesis 6:5; Romans 7:17-18, 8:6-8; Psalms 51:5)

The subconscious mind, often called the deep mind, operates on a level beneath our consciousness. This level houses what the Scriptures call the "heart of man" and is the control center of our soul. Our conscious mind and deep mind are connected, so, as our conscious mind processes what we learn and what happens to us, the result is filtered down into the subconscious mind and stored there. In the same way that our physical heart pumps life-giving blood throughout our bodies, what is contained in the deep mind affects our entire soul. This can cause all kinds of hidden troubles. Whatever is in the "heart of man," either good or evil, permeates the entire soul area and manifests in a variety of good and bad behaviors. Unfortunately, the sinful nature also resides in the heart of humankind, making it capable of doing terrible things. Jesus taught that it is not what we put into our bodies that defiles us; instead, it is what comes out of our hearts that causes us to sin. This is because it is in the "heart of man," located in the deep mind, that the sinful nature is lodged.

My first understanding of the sinful nature came to me in a dramatic way. I will never forget it. The Lord gave me a vision of myself standing on a narrow, unprotected bridge looking down into a vile and frightening abyss. I stood there hoping I would not fall in when the understanding came that the dark, vile thing I was looking into was my very own heart. I could only gasp out, "O Lord, I didn't know I was so awful!" He gently revealed to me that this horror was not a result of anything I had ever done, but that the sins and wrong things I do are a result of this awful thing living in me. The sinful nature is the part of us that God did not create. We inherited it when Adam and Eve fell into sin. Every baby born, with only one exception, has had this nature within.

The Will
(Relevant Scriptures: 2 Peter 1:21; Hebrews 11:24-25)

The will is the area of the soul that makes us independent and gives us the ability to determine our own course. God literally created us to make our own decisions, making us like Him, a free moral agent with a will of our own. This is the area of our soul God that will not touch unless invited and unless we choose His will over our own. We are completely free to choose to accept a relationship with our Creator through the salvation provided to us through Jesus, His Son. Or, we can rebel against Him, even until we are destroyed.

The will also provides the drive and perseverance to follow through with what we decide. During the years after my dad's death, as one crisis was met by another, my mother often said, "If there is a will, there is a way." This statement proved itself true many times for my family. Over my lifetime, those words have come to my rescue, leading me to persevere instead of give up. Once we know the Lord and seek to know His will for us, the personal will strengthens our ability to follow Him and His ways. Free will is a great and awe-inspiring gift. Without it, we would be puppets on a string. That was never God's will for us.

The Emotions

Our emotions are the thermometer of our soul. It is here that we have a full range of feelings, including love, fear, hate, anger, sadness, peace, and joy. Without our emotions, life would be void of passion and our motivation would be greatly diminished. There is no greater motivator than love, followed by anger, fear, and, sadly, hate. Our emotions are an indicator of what is going on in our hearts and minds. The will, when properly working, is a thermostat that helps develop our decisions, based on the intellectual reasoning of the information coming from the heart, mind, and senses. The emotions, however, simply react with feeling and passion to that same information. The will without emotion would make us dispassionate and boring. The emotions without the will would lead us astray with every nuance of feeling. We need both, in a healthy balance, to be vibrant, caring individuals.

Summary

The separation between the soul area and the spirit area played an important role in God's ability to interact with Adam and Eve before the fall. The most difficult problem God faced in dealing with the problems of the human spirit was His need to remain separate from it. The separation of the soul and spirit areas allowed Him enough of a covering so that He could dwell in the soul area of Adam and Eve without coming into direct contact with their individual spirits. In other words, He used the separation of the soul and spirit as a way to deal with His need to be separated from our wounded human spirits.

A common theory is that at the time of creation, God's Spirit and Adam's and Eve's spirits were fused together before the two created beings rebelled against God in the Garden of Eden. I now believe it more likely that God's Spirit resided in the deepest part of the soul known as the heart of humanity. When Adam and Eve were first created, God was able to live in their hearts, from where He attempted to communicate His love to their spirits, wooing them to know the truth about Him. This worked for a while, but confusion led to doubt—and then to rebellion when Adam and Eve ate the forbidden fruit. God was then forced to depart from the "heart of man," causing Him to be separated from their souls as well as from their individual spirits.

Whether you accept my belief that the separation of God's Spirit and our individual spirits took place in the spiritual-realm world before this world was created or you believe that this separation first took place in the Garden of Eden, Adam and Eve ended up in the same place, cast out of the Garden of Eden, mortally wounded and dead to the Spirit of God. And, they took all of humankind with them.

CHAPTER 6

THE FALL OF HUMANITY

(Relevant Scriptures: Genesis 2:8; Luke 2:52)

As God completed the creation of this natural-realm world, He declared it to be good, but when He looked upon His creation of Adam and Eve; He set them apart by declaring them to be very good. To this day, the part of us that God created is still very good; however, that part of us is now influenced and tainted by a foreign sinful nature that God did not create. How that nature came to reside in our souls was by way of the fall of humanity.

God the Father placed His beautiful created children in an equally beautiful place on Earth called the Garden of Eden. It was an idyllic place, in perfect harmony and full of peace and love, where Adam and Eve could be in communion with God. It is an earthly picture of God's heavenly kingdom before Lucifer fell. At this time, God's Spirit resided deep within the heart of their souls, communing with their spirits as best He could. It is likely that there were times when He appeared to them in a body so they could also relate to Him more easily with the conscious area of their minds. This was a special time between God and His first two created children as they communicated together.

We must understand that Adam and Eve had no conscious memories of the spiritual realm or of their former relationship with God. When we are born into the body, the spirit is not able to communicate the memories of the spiritual realm. These memories are there, deep within the spirit, and the spirit acts upon them. However, the conscious area of the mind is not aware of them. Even Jesus had to regain the consciousness of who He was as He grew in favor of God and humankind. It is the same growing experience for all of us, beginning with Adam and Eve. As far as they were concerned, their first memory of God was of the time spent in the lovely Garden of Eden.

Remember, it is my belief that the natural-realm world was created so that the spiritual-realm world could be restored. Adam and Eve were here on a mission to make a choice between God and Lucifer, now known as Satan. This choice would eventually dispel the confusion that had overtaken them in the spiritual-realm war. It is impossible to make an informed and permanent decision unless you understand the differences between your choices. The time spent with God in the garden gave Adam and Eve a chance to know Him more intimately and establish a relationship with Him. They would soon make a choice that would open the way for them to know the truth about Satan.

The Authority of Humanity
(Relevant Scriptures: Genesis 1:26–28; Matthew 28:18)

It is the great tragedy of humanity that every human born since the fall has inherited the sinful nature from Adam and Eve. How could it be that the actions of Adam and Eve caused the entire lineage of humankind to be affected in this way? The answer is found in the way in which God created Adam and Eve and in the irrevocable gifts He bestowed upon them at the time of creation.

There are only three uniquely created individuals, Adam, Eve, and Jesus; all others come into this world through the normal way of procreation. Adam was created first, formed by God's own hand. God then formed Eve by taking a rib from Adam, which gave the man and woman a special connection. Jesus, God's only begotten Son, was formed in the womb of the Virgin Mary as the Holy Spirit hovered over her. Each one of these special individuals had the power and authority to affect all of creation.

When God gave Adam and Eve dominion over His created world, along with the free will to rule, He gave them the authority to decide the course of this world. Authority has within it the responsibility for the decisions made under it. When, of their own free will, Adam and

Eve chose to ingest the forbidden fruit, the sinful nature became part of the inheritance of the entire human race. In addition, because all creation was under their dominion, all of creation was affected and the very atmosphere of this world changed and was thrown out of balance.

Two Trees
(Relevant Scriptures: Genesis 2:9, 15–17)

In the center of the garden grew two magnificent trees, the Tree of Life and the Tree of the Knowledge of Good and Evil. "The Tree of Knowledge and the Tree of Life are symbolic of two spiritual lineages or "family trees."(Rick Joyner, There were Two Trees in the Garden) These trees produced two very different fruits. Fruit is the result of the DNA of the tree. What is housed in the seed of the tree will determine the fruit. When we eat the fruit, we ingest into our bodies what is contained in that fruit. The choice given to Adam and Eve was represented by these two trees, and the consequences of their decision were determined by their fruit.

Tree of Life

The Tree of Life had within in it the Spirit of God. The fruit it produced was God's own nature, giving us the very righteousness of Christ Jesus. The seed of this fruit produced the life of God in us and life with God for all eternity. The fruit of this tree gives us a relationship with God as we depend on Him for our salvation. This is the fruit of the grace of God, which leads to everlasting life in His heavenly kingdom. It is not by accident that Jesus died on a cross made from a tree, for that cross truly symbolizes the Tree of Life and was used to open the way for our spiritual life in God.

Tree of the Knowledge of Good and Evil

The Tree of the Knowledge of Good and Evil contained the nature of Lucifer, later named Satan. The fruit it produced was the sinful nature of Lucifer, who believed that he was greater than God. He had become so aware of his own power and beauty that he rebelled against God, believing that he no longer needed Him. This forbidden fruit contained spiritual death, which is separation from God.

The Garden of Eden was filled with beautiful trees and plants, all with wonderful fruit for Adam and Eve's enjoyment. The only fruit they were not allowed to eat was the fruit of the Tree of the Knowledge of Good and Evil. God gave Adam and Eve a dire warning never to eat the fruit produced by this tree because it was poisonous. He went so far as to tell them that if they ate this fruit, they would surely die. As long as Adam and Eve observed this warning, life in the garden remained the same.

We have no idea how long Adam and Eve lived obediently in the Garden of Eden. We also do not know how many times Satan approached them in an effort to pressure them to eat the forbidden fruit. We can be sure that Satan was unrelenting in his pursuit of Adam and Eve, for his power was present in the forbidden fruit. God had given Adam and Eve dominion over His created realm, the same world Satan wanted to rule over. In order for Satan to rule over this world, he had to have control over Adam and Eve. We know that the day did come when Satan stirred up Eve's confusion, which was present deep within her spirit. He told her that if she ate the forbidden fruit, she would be like God. This is exactly the same deception Satan believed about himself. The temptation became too great for Eve, so, in one irrevocable act, she ate the forbidden fruit and then convinced Adam to do the same.

Ramifications of the Fall of Humanity
(Relevant Scripture: Genesis 3:1–7)

When Adam and Eve ate the forbidden fruit, they actually ingested into themselves the sinful nature of Satan. When the sinful nature entered the heart of humanity, it forced the Spirit of God instantly to depart from the heart area of the soul, leaving Adam and Eve completely separated from God. The Spirit of God did not separate Himself from Adam and Eve because He was angry, in order to punish them, or because they disobeyed Him. God's Spirit departed from Adam and Eve so as not to destroy His created children. The sinful nature of Satan was now living in their hearts, and the Spirit of God could no longer remain within their souls or their bodies. After the fall of humanity and before the resurrection of Jesus, no one had ever had the Holy Spirit living inside. The Holy Spirit always came upon people. This was when our bodies did the job that they were created to do: cover the sinful nature within us.

I cannot imagine the impact on Adam and Eve when God's Spirit departed and Satan's sinful nature entered their soul areas. It must have been horrifying for them. In one dreadful moment, the mind, emotions, will, and heart of humankind all became tainted by the invasion of the sinful nature. Adam and Eve began to experience a host of new emotions such as fear, anger, jealousy, lust, shame, and hate. The ramifications didn't stop there. The garden and the entire planet were thrown out of balance and started to change. I wonder how Adam and Eve reacted the first time they saw a lion rip apart a lamb. We do know that they stood there totally exposed, aware of their nakedness and trying to craft something out of fig leaves to cover themselves. They understood the enormity of the act they had committed, and they were filled with fear and shame. They had no idea what God might do to them, so they hid themselves, dreading the moment when He called their names and came looking for them.

God Responds
(Relevant Scriptures: Genesis 3:8–24; Ephesians 5:21–33; Psalms 23:4)

It was in the coolest part of the day when Adam and Eve heard God walking in the garden and calling their names. The fact that God came looking for them is evidence that He was going to handle them with tender loving care. If He had wanted to punish them, then He would not have returned to the garden. He'd have left them to deal with the results of their actions on their own. Instead, God sought them out and told them some of what the future now held as a result of their actions. In doing this, He was preparing them for what was ahead so that the shock of their new condition would not totally overwhelm them. It must have been a relief when Adam and Eve realized that God was not going to desert them but help them deal with this horrible new dilemma.

The very first exchange between God and Adam and Eve shows us the terrible change that had come over the two created people. When God asked Adam if he had eaten the forbidden fruit, Adam blamed the woman whom God had placed in the garden. In so doing, he was actually blaming God and Eve for his actions. Eve responded by blaming Satan. She was the first to use the excuse "The Devil made me do it."

God spoke to each participant of the fall in the order of their participation. He dealt first with Satan, informing him that there would always be enmity between him and the woman. God put Satan on notice with the dire warning that one day Eve's seed would crush his head. Satan may have believed that he had gained control over God's creation through Eve. However, what really happened was that Satan opened the way for his own destruction through one of Eve's descendants. These words must have been a balm to Eve's broken heart as she realized that womanhood was going to aid in the redemption of humanity and the destruction of Satan.

God next turned to Eve, telling her that childbirth would now be a painful event, but that she would nevertheless still desire her husband, who would rule over her. Perhaps the saddest thing for Eve was the tension that would now be part of her relationship with Adam. Until the fall, Adam and Eve ruled in perfect union with each other, but after the fall, the battle of the sexes began. It continues to this very day. The change in their relationship was a result of the sinful nature living within them, which was not the way God intended it to be. God had designed them to have equal authority, working in harmony to rule over all creation. The ingestion of the sinful nature changed the man–woman relationship.

Adam and Eve's souls were deeply affected by their failure to obey God. They passed this damage on to the souls of the men and women born after them. Somewhere deep in the male psyche is a mistrust of women because of what Eve led Adam to do. Eve's power over Adam and his love and need for her led him to disobey God. This caused him to view his love for her as a weakness, and he consequently lost his trust in her and in himself. I believe that a man's love for a woman scares him on a level of which he is not consciously aware. This brings about the sinful nature in men and their tendency to suppress and control women. On the other side, the female psyche lost the confidence it once had to lead. The result is that woman gave up her God-given authority and allowed man to suppress her. She has within her, just as God said, a deep desire for her husband and a longing for his love and approval. Yet deep in her soul, she blames him for not trying to stop her from taking that fatal step. This left behind in woman a hidden lack of respect for man. Thank God, as we grow in the Lord and in His ways, this damage is being repaired, but things are still out of balance between men and women.

The apostle Paul attempted to minister to men and women in this area, encouraging them to submit to one another. He instructed wives to respect their husbands and husbands to love their wives. For many men, the hardest thing to do is to express how deeply they love and need their wives. This is what Eve lost after the fall. It is also what the hearts of women most desire. On the other hand, women can sometimes be disrespectful toward their husbands. The respect of a wife is a need hidden deep within the male soul. It is sad that the things most important to the emotional health of a male–female relationship are what the sinful nature within our souls often subconsciously leads us to withhold. Submitting one to the other is simply loving and respecting each other and providing for each other's needs as best we can.

After dealing with Eve, God then turned His attention to Adam, preparing him for the changes he was going to experience. Adam had tended the garden before the fall when all was idyllic, but now the entire atmosphere of Earth was altered. The ground was going to produce weeds and pestilence, and the sky and oceans were going to produce destructive weather patterns. Cultivating the garden would now be backbreaking work for Adam. However, the most shocking thing was the revelation that Adam would return to the dust from which he had come. It was here that God prepared Adam and Eve for the death of their bodies. They were already dead to the Spirit of God, and now they learned that the death of their bodies would one day follow.

Death

Ever since the fall of Adam and Eve, the reality of death has been part of the human condition. The first death that Adam and Eve experienced happened immediately when God's Spirit separated from their hearts, making them dead to the Spirit of God. The second, physical death happened later when their individual spirits separated from their bodies.

When the world became a damaged, out-of-balance, sinful place, the atmosphere became a deadly place for the human body. The spirit and soul together control the body, so the soul's turmoil caused so much disharmony within the body that it became vulnerable to illness, pain, and injury. At the same time, pestilence and turmoil were loosed upon the earth, subjecting the body to all kinds of damage. The result is that the body finally bows to the unrelenting attack of this sinful atmosphere. The body dies, forcing the spirit to leave it behind.

We live our entire lives in the valley of the shadow of death. Each of us has to come to terms with the eventuality of our own death. In addition, the grief and separation we experience after the death of our loved ones is a devastating ramification of the fall. Death is among the most difficult for us to handle. It took me a long time to realize that death is not only a curse but is also a gift to this fallen world.

The ability to recognize the other side of death was another precious revelation. This one came to me in the form of a question: What if there were no death? I tried to imagine what life on Earth would be like without the existence of death. I came to realize that without the presence of death, this sin-ridden world would be an unbearable place to live. If nothing on Earth could die, then how would we control all the disease, pestilence, weeds, harmful bacteria, etc.? How would we possibly cope with the suffering of all those injured or diseased beyond our ability to heal? Death indeed has its job to do in this fallen world full of suffering. Death is often the only door through which to escape what would otherwise be endless suffering. The truth is, without death, life on Earth would be a living hell. Praise God that Jesus, through His death on the cross, transformed death for all who are in Him into a gateway to everlasting life in His heavenly kingdom. It is through the death of the body that we are finally free to return home to the spiritual-realm world.

Life in the garden of Eden had clearly changed. The proof that death was already a part of those changes is in God's having made garments of animal skins for Adam and Eve. He banished them from the garden and placed on the east side some cherubim and a flaming sword flashing back and forth to guard the way to the Tree of Life. They had already disobeyed God once, and He would not risk their doing it again. In their sinful condition, eating the fruit from the Tree of Life was no longer possible and would result in their complete destruction. Humankind would not be able to eat from the Tree of Life until the time when a solution for their sinful condition was supplied.

Recap

(Relevant Scriptures: Deuteronomy 30:19–20; Joshua 24:15; 2 Samuel 14:14)

What happened in the garden after the fall of Adam and Eve did not surprise God. Indeed, He was waiting for it to happen because His spiritual children had already disobeyed and rebelled against Him in the spiritual-realm world. The ramifications of the fall of Adam and Eve were very similar to those in the spiritual-realm world. Whatever flaw or confusion had affected the spiritual realm's citizens was present in Adam and Eve as they lived in the garden. This meant that it was only a matter of time before they rebelled against God.

Adam and Eve were in the garden to make a choice, and God supplied that choice through the fruit of two trees. God had created this world of form and matter in order to undo the damage that had been done to them and to the spiritual world that was their home. They were on a mission of their own redemption and healing, to dispel the confusion that had taken root in their spirits. The main focus of this mission was to make a final and informed decision about whom they would believe and whom they would follow. To do this, Adam and Eve had to clearly understand the difference between God and Satan. It is through the fall that they came to understand the true nature of Satan. When Satan's sinful nature entered Adam and Eve's souls, they immediately understood the gravity of their decision and the frightening difference between the nature of God and the nature of Satan.

It is the same choice each individual who is born into this world has to make. The only difference between our situation and theirs is that we are born with the sinful nature inside us and have to learn to know the sweet, loving nature of God. The ways of the sinful nature come naturally to us, but we have to learn to decide to follow God's ways. It is through the consequences of sin that we are often driven to seek the grace of God. Once we know the wages of sin, the love and grace of God is the most precious thing we can obtain. He truly is the pearl of great price.

The nature of God and the nature of Satan will never be able to coexist. As long as the two exist, there will be no permanent peace on Earth. Nor can the spiritual-realm world be whole again until Satan, the source of evil, is defeated. This cannot be accomplished until every citizen of the spiritual realm has been given the opportunity to make a clear and final decision between God and Satan. Adam and Eve made the first fatal choice to disobey God and eat the forbidden fruit. However, this was not the final choice. As they stood in the garden before God, He was already preparing them to make a second choice.

A Hidden Plan

When we take a closer look at the Scriptures discussing how God dealt with Adam and Eve in the garden, we can discern His pattern for the redemption of His people. Hidden within God's loving actions is already the outline of His plan to save His fallen children. Genesis 3:8–9 tells us that God came to the garden seeking Adam and Eve; thus, *salvation will come from God*. In verses 10–13, God holds them accountable for their actions; consequently, *we are accountable for our sin* and *will be required to confess of our sinfulness*. In verses 14–19, God informed them of the consequences of their actions, revealing that *sin will have serious consequences*. In verse 21, God made garments of animal skins for Adam and Eve; therefore, *God will provide the covering of our sin that will enable humankind to come into His presence again*. Also, *this covering will require the shedding of blood*. In verses 22–24, God banishes them from the garden to protect them, confirming that *even in our sinful condition; God will protect and provide for us. He will never desert us.*

What kind of love is this? Even when we have disobeyed God, causing havoc and suffering beyond our ability to comprehend, He still comes to rescue and save, not to punish and destroy. God had that kind of love for us in the garden of Eden, and He loves us the same way today, for it is "while we are yet sinners" (Romans 5:8) that He comes to us with the way of salvation. It was true then, and it is true to this very day. We need only to stand before Him just as Adam and Eve did, confess our sin, and accept His way of salvation.

Section Two

GOD'S SOLUTION

CHAPTER 7

THE ROLE OF THE BODY IN THE PLAN OF SALVATION

(Relevant Scriptures: Genesis 2:7; Luke 24:36–39; John 20:19; John 3:5–6)

The role the body plays in God's salvation plan is one more thing that convinces me that God created this world to work out the problems already existing in the spiritual realm. The body is critical to the plan of salvation. This natural-realm world was created so that our individual spirits could reside in bodies of living flesh. The body enabled God to accomplish salvation in a way that would have been impossible in the spiritual realm, which is our home. This is because the spiritual realm exists in an entirely different dimension from the natural-realm world. The bodies there are fit for the heavenly realms and are not made of solid matter. Nor do they operate in the same way our earthly bodies do.

Once Jesus was in His resurrected body, He was able to enter rooms with locked doors and also appear instantly in different places. To provide what was needed for our salvation, God needed a barrier or a covering that was strong enough to protect our spirit and soul from coming into direct contact with Him. If it had been possible for God to supply that covering in the spiritual-realm world, then He would have done so. Instead, He provided the necessary covering by creating a physical world and a body of flesh to house the spirit and the soul. It is likely that without the creation of this natural-realm world and the body of flesh, the separation between God and His spiritual-realm citizens would have been permanent. The human body is certainly not what saved us; however, it is definitely a tool God used to save us.

Jesus made a profound and multilayered statement in a conversation He had with a Pharisee named Nicodemus. Jesus said, "I tell you the truth, no one can enter the kingdom of God unless he is born of water and the Spirit. Flesh gives birth to flesh, but the Spirit gives birth to spirit" (John 3:5–6). Some understand this verse to be about baptism by water and baptism by the Spirit. However, if we look at closely, we discover that Jesus is not speaking about baptism; He is referring to our physical birth. We are born of the flesh when we enter the birth canal after the water breaks. He then speaks of a second birth, when we are born again of God's Spirit. This spiritual birth occurs only after our physical birth and when we accept Jesus as Savior. It was a magical moment of revelation when I realized what Jesus was actually saying in these verses. I have come to believe that to be born again of the Spirit of God, our individual spirit must come to Earth by being born into a body—and then it is possible for us to be born again of God's Spirit. In other words, we must first be born of the flesh so that we can be reunited with God's Spirit.

The Body Contains the Spirit and the Soul

The most basic function of the natural-realm world and the body is to contain. God designed the earth to contain the massive problems of the spiritual realm in a smaller, physical world. This allowed Him to work out the problems of the spiritual realm over a period of time. God then used the body as a container in a number of ways. He first contained the flawed spirits of Adam and Eve in bodies, providing them with a living protective covering that would enable Him to be in closer contact with them than would have been possible in the spiritual-realm world. He blessed them with a mission to increase in number, fill the Earth, subdue it, and rule over all other creatures. The calling to increase in number and fill the earth was given to Adam and Eve as male and female, together as partners and as one unit for the purpose of procreation. In other words, Adam and Eve were called to begin the process of creating bodies for other spiritual-realm citizens waiting to make their way into this world.

To this day, there is disagreement about when the human spirit enters the body. Some argue that it is at the moment of conception; others believe that it is at the moment of birth. If I recall correctly, there are those who believe that this occurs at some point during a fetus' development. I have no idea when our spirits enter our bodies. However, for the purpose of salvation and being reunited with the Spirit of God, it is absolutely necessary for our spirits to take on flesh and journey to this world. God started this process when He created the bodies of Adam and Eve. He then continued the process of creating bodies of flesh through Adam and Eve and their descendants. In so doing, He was making a way for all of His spiritual-realm children who were affected by Lucifer's fall to come to Earth, giving them the opportunity to overcome the problems in their spirits and souls.

The body supplied the covering for our individual spirits, both before and after the fall of Adam and Eve. Before the fall, God's Spirit could reside in the heart area, deep inside the soul of Adam and Eve. This was possible because the soul and the spirit were housed in separate areas, which provided the protection God needed so that His Spirit would not come into direct contact with human beings' flawed spirits. However, once the sinful nature entered the soul area, the Spirit of God could no longer remain and was forced to depart. At that point, the body continued to provide the needed covering for the sinful nature, which allowed the Holy Spirit to maintain contact with humankind—but now only from outside the body.

The Body Is the Container for the Sinful Nature
(Relevant Scriptures: Romans 7:18; Psalms 85:2)

After Adam and Eve fell, the body became the container for the sinful nature, which became part of the flesh. Even though this was the result of Adam and Eve's dreadful decision—one that marked a tragic moment for all of humankind—it was a necessary step in God's plan of salvation. God knew the questions and doubts that Adam and Eve held deep in their spirits. He was also aware that it was just a matter of time before Satan would use their doubts to trick them into eating the forbidden fruit, allowing the sinful nature to become the inheritance of all of humanity. Adam and Eve were responsible for their own disobedience, but God was determined to rescue them from the tragedy of the fall in the spiritual realm and from their individual fall. Everything went just the way God knew it would. He had a plan of His own to undo the damage.

Once the sinful nature became part of the human soul, it was lodged in a place where the sinless nature of Christ could one day begin the process of destroying it and freeing humankind from sin. I imagine that when Satan tricked Eve and Adam into ingesting the forbidden fruit and the sinful nature entered the heart of humanity's soul, he thought that he had won a great battle against God. Instead, Satan just opened the way for his own destruction and the death of the sinful nature. Jesus, the very Way of salvation, was waiting in heaven to come save the world, for He was predestined before the foundations of this world were laid to be the Savior of all humankind.

The Body Contains the Fullness of God
(Relevant Scriptures: Colossians 2:9–12; Galatians 4:4–5; Hebrews 2:14–15)

The most crucial reason why God created the body was so that He could become one with humankind and take on the flesh. This enabled Jesus to answer the demands of the law, which was one of the obstacles that had to be overcome. After Lucifer fell in the spiritual realm and, later, Adam and Eve fell in the natural realm, humankind was completely helpless, with no way to undo—and no hope of undoing—the results of these two events. If God and humanity were going to be reunited, then it was going to be done by an act of God. However, it was impossible for God to supply the atonement for sin required by the law. God, the Father can never sin. The same is true for God, the Holy Spirit and Jesus, the Son of God. The Godhead is holy, righteous, and completely without sin and the ability to sin. There is absolutely no way that God could atone for the sins of humankind because He simply was not responsible for the sin. It was humanity that had sinned. Only someone who was part of humankind could have the ability to atone for those sins and satisfy the demands of the law.

God, the Father overcame this obstacle by joining together the full nature of God and the full nature of humanity in one perfect, unique individual. When God was born into a body of flesh, He became one with humanity. This gave Him all the power and authority to atone for the sin of humankind. In the same way, Adam and Eve had the power to affect all humankind, and, likewise, all humankind fell because of their actions. Jesus had the same power to affect all humankind. By accepting His actions on our behalf, we receive the atonement for sin and are reunited with the Spirit of God. If Jesus could not have become all Man, then there would be no Savior and no Way for us to be reunited with God's Spirit. We would have remained dead in our sin, separated from God forever. It was through the body of flesh that the incarnation of God and Man was made possible.

The Body Is Temporal
(Relevant Scriptures: 1Corinthians 15:42-44, 54-55; Romans 14:8; John 11:25-26)

Another reason why the body is such a critical tool in the plan of salvation is because it is temporal and will die. To get a deeper understanding, we must revisit the definition of *death*. *Separation* is the basic meaning of the word *death*. This separation occurs on two levels. The first level is "Natural death; end of the life of the body." (Smith's Bible

Dictionary) The natural-realm death of the human body happens when the individual spirit separates from the body. However, because the human spirit is eternal the death of the body does not mean that we no longer exist. The only part of a human being that dies and becomes nonexistent is the body; it returns to the dust of the earth from which it came. When our earthly body dies, we get a new, resurrected body fit for the atmosphere of the spiritual realm.

"Spiritual death; is alienation from God." (Smith's Bible Dictionary) Spiritually speaking when we are connected to God, we are spiritually alive in God. When we are not connected to God's Spirit, we are spiritually dead, or separated from God. The spiritual-realm law demands a death sentence for rebellion against God. This is not a law that God commands us to follow and holds over His spiritual citizens to keep them in line. Instead, it is the systemic condition of the spiritual-realm world. God is Spirit, and the world God lives in is spiritual. In the spiritual world, if anything sinful or imperfect comes in direct contact with the full glory of God, it is instantly destroyed. This happens not by the deliberate actions of God or even by the design of God; rather, it is simply a condition of the nature of His being, His holiness, and His glory.

The environment of the spiritual realm did not provide what was needed to accomplish the task of undoing the damage done there. To overcome the problem of spiritual death (separation from God), the sin and imperfection of the spiritual realm citizens had to be eliminated. God had the awing task of making sinless that which was sinful and perfect that which was imperfect. God chose to do this within the confinement of temporary bodies living in a temporary world.

He used the body to contain the problem, which is the sinful nature lodged in our souls. Then, through the virgin birth, the sinless soul and Spirit of Jesus was born into a body of flesh. This enabled Jesus to satisfy the death penalty for sin by dying Himself, sparing human beings from destruction. Since the sinful nature is contained in human bodies and all that is needed for salvation was contained in the body of Jesus, the body gave Jesus the means to accomplish the atonement for the sin of all humankind. In other words, the death of Jesus' body was the sacrifice that would satisfy the death penalty required by law. Once the sacrifice was made, the way was open for our individual spirits to be made alive in God through the reunion of our spirits and His. Atonement for sin is activated in each individual through his or her own personal choice to accept Jesus as Savior. It is only through Christ's sacrifice that the sinful nature is destroyed and human reunion with the Spirit of God is made possible.

A Closing Thought

The role of the body is fascinating to me. It is an important part in the plan of salvation. I have no doubt that our time in a body is necessary for our salvation. Our bodies are where the sinful nature is lodged and where our individual spirits reside. It is through Christ's sacrifice of His body that the forgiveness of sin is made possible, thereby giving us the opportunity to accept His sacrifice for our sin and receive the covering over the sinful nature that allows us to be reunited with the Holy Spirit of God, finally putting to death the sinful nature within each of us. There is one additional role the body will play in the future. I do not totally understand it, but one day, Satan is going to be born into a body and the person known as the Antichrist will come into this world. The implication of this is enormous. I suspect it will be the final stage of Satan's demise.

CHAPTER 8

WHAT IS SO SPECIAL ABOUT JESUS?

(Relevant Scriptures: Genesis 1:1–2; Luke 1:34–35; Luke 2:52)

I cannot remember a time when I didn't believe that Jesus was the Son of God and the Savior of the world. I don't believe I ever seriously doubted those truths. I just couldn't comprehend how it worked, so, of course, I had questions. One of my more nagging questions was how is it that Jesus could die for my sins? During the Christmas season, I would ponder another question: Why did Jesus have to come as a baby? It seemed to me that Jesus' having been born into this world in the same way we are causes people to doubt that He truly is the Son of God. I thought that something a bit more spectacular would have worked better. Most of my questions can be summed up in one: What is so special about Jesus that He could die for the sins of all humankind?

Jesus Is All God and All Man

(Relevant Scriptures: John 1:14; Matthew 17:5; Mark 1:9–11, 15:39; Colossians 2:9; 1 Timothy 2:5, 3:16; 1 John 5:20; Philippians 2:8)

Part one of God's plan of salvation began when the Spirit of God hovered over the waters as He formed this natural-realm world. Part two of God's plan of salvation began when the Holy Spirit hovered over the Virgin Mary, forming in her womb the most unique individual ever to be born into this natural-realm world. In the body of this baby growing in His mother's womb lived the lineages of two distinct natures. From the Virgin Mary, Jesus inherited the full nature of humanity, the very nature from which we need redemption. Being Himself the only Son of God, He already possessed the full nature of God, the very nature that would save the other. The divine nature and the human nature were united in Jesus, forming one undivided and indivisible person. Thus, He became the bridge between the spiritual-realm world and the natural-realm world.

The breathtaking reality is that when we accept Jesus as our Savior, the same miracle that took place in Him occurs in us. We, once again, come into personal union with the Spirit of God. He dwells within the heart area of our soul and is fused with our individual spirit. What God the Father first accomplished in Jesus enables Him to accomplish through Jesus the same thing in those who accept Jesus as their Savior.

Jesus Has All Authority in Heaven and on Earth
(Relevant Scriptures: Matthew 9:4–6, 28:18; John 5:27, 17:2–5; Romans 9:5; Genesis 1:28)

It is because Jesus is all God and completely Man that He received the authority to have an effect on both the spiritual-realm world and the natural-realm world. Being God, Jesus already possessed all the power, glory, and attributes that belonged to Him through His eternal position in the Godhead. Likewise, when Jesus took on flesh and became all Man, He also became the recipient of the dominion and authority God had bestowed on Adam and Eve at the time of creation. This is important because it enabled Jesus to reclaim authority over the natural-realm world that God the Father had given to humankind through Adam and Eve. If Jesus had not had this authority, then His life, death, and resurrection could not have affected this natural-realm world and accomplished the salvation of humanity.

Jesus not only inherited the authority given to Adam and Eve, but He also came under the same judgment, the same laws, and the same penalty of death as the rest of us. In other words, His was a twofold inheritance. On one hand, He received the same authority God had given to Adam and Eve to affect all humankind. On the other hand, He became responsible for the actions of Adam and Eve and the sin that followed. This made it possible for Jesus to repent and atone for the sins of all humanity. In this way, God overcame the problem that it was humankind who had sinned and that only humankind could repent and be responsible for that sin. When Jesus took on the flesh and became one with humankind, it opened the Way for us to inherit the forgiveness of sin, life everlasting, and reconciliation with God through Jesus' sacrifice—in the same way we inherited the sinful nature through Adam and Eve.

Jesus Is the Second Adam
(Relevant Scriptures: Romans 5:12–21; 1 Corinthians 15:20–22, 45–49; Genesis 2:7, 3:6–7, 21–23)

The Scriptures refer to Jesus as the second Adam. To get a clear understanding of how Jesus could succeed where Adam and Eve had failed, we have to know the differences between the first Adam and Jesus, the second Adam. Keep in mind that Adam, Eve, and Jesus are the only three uniquely created individuals that have the power to alter all of humankind by exercising the authority that God the Father had given them. However, in this section, we will concentrate on the first Adam and on Jesus, the second Adam.

One of the main differences between Adam and Jesus is the way they came into this world. In the first phase of the plan of salvation, God placed Adam and Eve in a body of flesh He formed from dust with His own hand. Then, God the Father breathed physical life into their bodies, giving them a living house to hold their individual spirits. Jesus, however, was not made; He was begotten.

In other words, Jesus was not created as Adam was; He grew in Mary's womb and was born through her birth canal, in the same way we all come into this world. The breathtaking difference between a normal birth and Jesus' birth is that He was conceived without a human father. Through this Immaculate Conception, God was no longer merely harbored in humanity's soul, nor was He simply sitting on the throne of humanity's heart, as He was in Adam and Eve before the fall. In Jesus, God became one with humanity and had taken on its flesh.

This knowledge answered another one of my old, nagging questions: Why did Jesus have to come as a baby? To become all Man, He had to take on the flesh in the same way we all do. He had to be born into it, and that could be accomplished only through a woman's womb. To be the Son of God, Jesus had to be born without the aid of a human father. Remember what God told Satan in the garden after the fall: It is through the offspring of the woman that the head of Satan will one day be crushed. God did not mention that Adam would play a part in providing the offspring that would one day destroy Satan. Jesus is that offspring.

The two ways in which the first Adam and Jesus, the second Adam, came into this world is not the only difference between them. We all have a spirit and a soul housed in a body. So it was with Adam and Jesus. The difference between them is that housed in the spirit area of the first Adam was his own individual spirit. He was the spiritual-realm citizen whom God had chosen as the first to come to Earth housed in a body. Jesus, on the other hand, is the second person of the Godhead, fully God along with God the Father and God the Holy Spirit. Housed in Jesus' spirit area was the very Spirit of God, making Jesus fully God.

One major way in which Adam (and Eve) and Jesus are the same is that they came into this world without the sinful nature already harbored in their soul areas. As long as Adam and Eve did not eat the forbidden fruit, they did not ingest Satan's sinful nature. Once they ate the fruit, the sinful nature entered their soul areas and became part of all humankind. Even though Jesus was all Man with the full inheritance of humanity, He was born without the sinful nature in His soul.

The question then becomes this: How is it possible that Jesus, born of Mary, did not have the sinful nature? The short answer is found in the way in which Jesus was conceived: without the aid of a human father. To get a better grasp of how this worked, we must go back to the creation of Adam and Eve. Adam was the first to be created. Until Eve was created, the seed of all humankind was contained in Adam alone. When God created Eve, He separated a part of Adam to form Eve. Although they were completely separate individuals, they were designed to come together to make one union for the purpose of procreation. To create a human being took Adam's seed implanted in Eve's egg. The two then formed a human embryo. I find it interesting that the fall of humankind did not take place until Eve gave Adam the forbidden fruit to eat. Eve's eyes were not opened until Adam had also eaten the forbidden fruit. It took both Adam and Eve to eat the fruit for the sinful nature to enter the heart of all humankind. I believe this is a key to understanding how Jesus could be born of the flesh without inheriting the sinful nature. It would have taken the seed of a descendant of Adam coming together with the egg of a descendant of Eve for the sinful nature to reside in Jesus. In other words, it would have taken both male and female to pass on the inheritance of the sinful nature. Jesus was conceived through the power of God; Adam's seed was not involved. Thus, Jesus was born without the sinful nature living in His soul. He was born without sin. And, because He is God, His nature is incapable of sinning. He truly is the spotless Lamb of God.

Although Jesus did not have the sinful nature in Him, He did have the desires of the flesh and the weak human nature that comes with being all Man. Because He was also all God, His weak human nature was fortified by the strength and power of the Holy Spirit of God. This enabled Jesus to resist every temptation to sin, whether the temptations came directly from Satan or from the desires of the flesh. When we contrast the temptation that Adam and Eve had to resist with the amount of temptation that Jesus had to endure, it becomes apparent that Jesus resisted the temptation to sin every moment of His life. He never failed. For Adam and Eve to resist Satan's temptations and remain free of the sinful nature, they needed to obey one of God's commandments. I find it breathtaking that Jesus had to resist Satan's temptations for the entire thirty-three years He lived on Earth, up until the moment He died on the cross. The first Adam, along with Eve, failed in his birthright, but Jesus, the second Adam, would not and did not fail.

CHAPTER 9

JESUS IS THE ARK OF THE COVENANT

(Relevant Scriptures: Genesis 6:9–22; Exodus 25:10–22; Hebrews 9:4–5, 11:7; Deuteronomy 10:5; Numbers 17:1–13; Leviticus 16:34; 2 Corinthians 1:20)

If the word *separation* can be used to describe what happened when humanity fell, then the word *containment* is the description for one of the methods God used to carry out His plan to end the separation. My understanding of this came in another light-bulb moment when I finally realized that Jesus is the ark of the covenant, which God made with people so they could be saved. Jesus is the everlasting and final ark of God. However, before Jesus, there were two other important arks of God. The first one was Noah's ark, and the second was the nation of Israel's ark of the covenant. When we look closely at these early arks of God, we can see the similarities between them and Jesus.

The simplest definition of an ark is that it is a container. However, when it is a container of God, it is meant for a specific use. He designed its details.

Noah's ark was built according to very precise measurements and plans God had given to Noah. It was a huge ship that easily held all the animals, along with Noah and his entire family. Over time, the people of Earth had become so evil that God destroyed them in a flood. He used this ark to preserve His animal kingdom and the one family that had chosen to believe Him and live godly lives. It was this God-designed ark that saved Noah and his family. Likewise, it is Jesus who is the living ark of God, sent to save all who will believe in Him and accept Him as their Savior. Every person and animal in Noah's ark was saved, and everyone who is in Christ Jesus will also be saved and protected by God. They will not perish but will spend eternity in the safety of His care.

Another ark that was specifically designed by God was Israel's ark of the covenant. It was a beautiful portable chest made of acacia wood and covered with gold, inside and out. On the cover at each end sat a cherubim made of hammered gold, each facing the other and looking down at the cover. This ark was designed to hold Israel's holiest historical artifacts. It also served as a symbol of God's presence among the Israelites.

God used the Ark of the Covenant in three ways. The first was to serve as a container for the stone tablets inscribed with the law of Moses; a jar of manna that God had provided for the Israelites as they roamed in the wilderness; and the staff which budded to confirm Aaron's call to the priesthood. The ark's cover provided the second function: the place where sacrificial blood was spilled once a year on the Day of Atonement for the forgiveness of all the sins of the Israelites. The ark of God was also considered the focal point of God's presence with his people, which is its third function. God had promised Moses, "There above the cover between the two cherubim--I will meet with you." (Exodus 25:22) To restate, the ark of the covenant contained the law, manna from heaven, confirmation of the priesthood of God, and sacrificial blood for the forgiveness of sins—and it was a symbol of the direct, intimate presence of God. God gave this chest to His people as a reminder of what He had done for them and that He was with them. While all other tribes and nations struggled under ignorance and sin, God chose the Israelites to carry an ark that had within it the very beginnings of God's reconciliation with humanity. The Israelites were to be the enlightened, blessed people who would lead people of other nations to seek God.

The chest known as the ark of the covenant, or the ark of God, was destroyed along with the temple in Jerusalem in 586 BC. God never gave instructions to build a replacement. Instead, He personally designed the most intricate and unique container to house His very presence along with all that was needed to fulfill His covenant with humanity. He sent Jesus, His only Son, to be the one true living ark of the covenant. Note the similarities between what was kept in the chest of the ark of the covenant and what is contained in Jesus. In Christ Jesus, we have the fulfillment of all the promises God made to—and the covenants He made with—humankind. Jesus fulfills God's Word given through the prophets, He also fulfills the law. Jesus is the manna from heaven, predestined before the foundation of the world was laid to be the Savior of humanity. He is also the High Priest of the new covenant who intercedes for us at the throne of God. Just as, every year, the sacrificial blood of animals was shed over the Old Testament ark of the covenant for the forgiveness of the Israelites' sins, Jesus' blood was shed once for the forgiveness of the sins of all humankind.

Jesus Is the Fulfillment of the Law
(Relevant Scriptures: Matthew 5:17–18; Luke 24:44; Romans 3:21–24, 10:1–13; 2 Corinthians 5:21; Philippians 3:7–9)

Jesus, the final Ark of the Covenant, contains the fulfillment of what the historical objects represented. "To fulfill" something means "to execute; carry out; complete by performance" (The Grosset Webster Dictionary) The best example of fulfillment are the two stone tablets of the law known as the Ten Commandments.

When the law was given to the Jewish people, God no longer dwelled within His created children. He could influence humankind only from outside people's souls and bodies. His laws were an external method of controlling the sinful nature within the soul area of humankind until the time came when God's Spirit could reunite with our individual spirits. It is through the law that God provided the standard of righteousness and a means to contain sinful behavior.

Jesus made two seemingly contradictory statements regarding the law. He declared that He did not come to abolish the law or change one iota of it. He informed us that He came to fulfill the law. There is a huge difference between abolishing something and fulfilling it. If Jesus had declared the law abolished, then the law would have been revoked, resulting in the cancellation of the standard of righteousness. This would be the same as saying that sin no longer mattered. The standard would be gone. Forgiveness never declares sin to be acceptable. This is true when we forgive others, and it is especially true when Jesus came to bring forgiveness and salvation to us. Abolishing the law would have declared that which is wrong to be right, and that can never be done. Jesus never declared sinful behavior to be acceptable; instead, He declared the sinner forgiven and accepted. The judgment against sin will stand until the final battle, when sin will no longer exist. Until then, not one dot of the law will be changed.

To understand what it means that Jesus came to fulfill the law, we must first look at the intent of the law.

Righteousness is the goal of the law, so our righteousness is the fulfillment of the law. When Jesus informed us that He came to fulfill the law, He was telling us the incredibly good news that He came to make us righteous. He came to do for us what we are unable to do for ourselves. It is the righteousness of God dwelling within us that makes us righteous. No matter how well you kept the law before you were a Christian, and no matter how well you keep it after you become a Christian, it is still only the righteousness of Christ that can fully satisfy the demands of the law.

Jesus Is the Manna from Heaven
(Relevant Scripture: Exodus 16:1-36; John 6:25-40, 49-51)

Manna was a sweet, flake-like substance that rained down from heaven and settled on the desert ground in the same way as the morning dew. Just like the morning dew, it melted away each day under the heat of the sun. The manna appeared in the morning to feed the Israelites as they journeyed from Egypt to the Promised Land. Manna had supernatural characteristics. Only the amount needed for the day was to be gathered each morning, and each day the Israelites would make bread from the manna. If they attempted to store manna, it would develop maggots and produce a foul odor before the next day. This was true for five of the seven days; however, on the sixth day, the

Israelites were allowed to gather enough manna for that day and also for the Sabbath, the next day. The manna never rained down from heaven on the Sabbath, and the extra manna gathered on the sixth day stayed fresh to eat on the Sabbath. The Bible is explicit: Manna is a food that came directly from God.

God instructed Moses to fill a jar with the manna and keep it for the generations to come so they could see the bread He gave them to eat in the desert. Moses kept the jar of manna in the ark as a reminder of God's sustaining care for His people. It was with the daily manna that God fed and sustained the physical lives of His people as they journeyed through the desert. One of the lines in the Lord's Prayer is, "Give us each day our daily bread," which asks God to do for us, as we travel through this world, what He did for the Israelites when they roamed through the desert.

When Jesus declared Himself to be the true bread from heaven, He was relating Himself to the supernatural manna from God the Father. Jesus said,

> I am the bread of life. Your forefathers ate the manna in the desert, yet they died. But here is the bread that comes down from heaven, which a man may eat and not die. I am the living bread that came down from heaven. If anyone eats of this bread, he will live forever. This bread is my flesh, which I will give for the life of the world. (John 6:48–51)

It was through the death of His body that Jesus satisfied the demands of the law. In so doing, He opened the way for the Spirit of God to be reconciled with the individual spirits of people.

Once again, we see the act of ingesting food into the body. It was the forbidden fruit that contained Satan's sinful nature. When Adam and Eve ate the fruit, they brought the sinful nature into their bodies and souls. Everything necessary for the Spirit of God to reunite with the individual spirits of people is contained in Christ Jesus. When we ask Jesus, the bread of spiritual life, to be our Savior and come into our hearts, we are taking into ourselves the very Spirit of God, the only Way God has provided to save our souls. God supplied manna, a supernatural food, to feed the physical needs of the Israelites. He sent Jesus, the supernatural Bread of Life, to provide the Way for our spirits to reunite with the Spirit of God. In this, He ended humanity's separation from God, which is spiritual death, and made us spiritually alive in Himself.

Jesus Is the High Priest of the New Covenant
(Relevant Scripture: Hebrews 7–8)

There are times when I see God's sense of humor, especially in making sure that He gets His message across to His people. The story of Aaron's rod is one of those times. People were rebelling against Moses and Aaron as leaders during a time of discord and confusion about who was to be in charge. God had lost all patience with it. So, He instructed Moses to have each leader of the various tribes of Israel bring his staff to the tent of meeting. Then, God instructed Moses to write each tribe leader's name on his own staff. Aaron's name was to be written on the staff of the tribe of Levi. All twelve staffs were to be placed before the ark of the covenant. God promised that the staff of the man He chose to be the high priest would bud before morning. The rods were made of wood and, I'm sure, were well-worn and too old to sprout even a single bud. When morning came, Aaron's rod made of almond wood had not only sprouted but also budded, blossomed, and produced almonds, leaving not one shred of doubt as to whom God had chosen to be the high priest.

Through Aaron's rod, God confirmed Aaron's call to the priesthood. In this way, God chose men of the tribe of Levi to be the priests in charge of the sanctuary. God told Moses to place Aaron's rod in front of the ark so it would serve as a sign to the rebellious, saying that this would put an end to their grumbling against Him so they would not die. This is another example of God's protecting His people from the consequences of their sin. Let's remember that anything sinful or imperfect cannot come into contact with the direct presence of God without a protective covering. Until such a time as God provided a permanent protection, He used the method of the priesthood as one way to cover His people. It was a way to help them deal with their sinful state, teach them obedience, and allow them to come to know God. This is a perfect example of God's revealing to people that they needed an intercessor between themselves and Him. The high priest was the only one who could enter the area of the tabernacle holding the ark of the covenant without being put to death. Every year, the high priest would spill sacrificial blood over the ark's cover to make atonement for the sins of all Israelites.

Jesus is the fulfillment of the calling of the Aaronic priesthood. However, Jesus was not to be the high priest of the old covenant of the law as Aaron was; instead, He would be the High Priest of the new covenant of grace through the shedding of His own blood. Jesus was not from the tribe of Levi but was a High Priest fashioned after an earlier Old Testament priest who was also a king. Melchizedek was king of Salem, an early name for the city of Jerusalem. Melchizedek was also a priest of God Most High. His name means "king of righteousness" and "king of peace." According to Scripture, he was without father or mother, without genealogy, and without beginning of days or end of life; like the Son of God, he remained a priest forever. The Scripture declares Jesus to be a priest in the Order of Melchizedek—not a priest because of a decree regarding His ancestry, but on the basis of the power of His everlasting life.

In other words, Jesus is the eternal King of Kings as well as the eternal High Priest who intercedes for us before God's throne and atones for all our sins. In the same way that the Old Testament priest atoned for sin in the inner sanctum of the tabernacle over the ark of the covenant, Jesus is the High Priest who entered the Holy of Holies and opened the Way for us to enter, as well. He is the completion of the old covenant of the law, and He is the High Priest of the new covenant of grace.

Jesus Is the Sacrificial Lamb of God
(Relevant Scriptures: John 1:29–34; Hebrews 9, 10:1–18)

In the same way that God personally designed Noah's ark and the ark of the covenant to achieve His specific purposes, He designed Jesus, the living ark of the covenant, to be the Savior of the world. Jesus' body was the ark that contained everything needed to fulfill God's plan of salvation, including the sacrificial blood to atone for all the sins of humanity. Jesus was supernaturally conceived through the Holy Spirit and born without the sinful nature harbored in the area of His soul. This made Him the spotless, sinless, sacrificial Lamb of God. It was through the biological death of Jesus' body the spilling of His sacrificial blood that His body fulfilled its highest purpose. This was also the ultimate reason why God created the body.

The shedding of Jesus' sacrificial blood provided atonement for our sins. God's forgiveness of our sins is the result of Christ's atonement. To grasp the full impact of what this means, we must discuss the words *atonement, forgiveness, covering,* and *seal.*

Atonement

"*Atonement* means expiation; reparation; to expiate is to redeem; reparation is paid for loss or damage. (The Grosset Webster Dictionary) It is the final payment that fully satisfies the debt. The law of the spiritual realm demanded a death sentence as penalty for rebellion against God. The wage of sin is death, so the only way to atone for the sins of humankind was through death. Life is in the blood, so, when Jesus died on the cross to atone for the sins of the world, His blood sacrifice covered the sins of all humankind. His blood settled the penalty required by the law. In Christ's death, the debt owed for the rebellion against God was paid and the forgiveness of sin was accomplished.

Forgiveness
(Relevant Scriptures: Ephesians 1:7–8, 2:13; Colossians 1:13–14)

"*Forgiveness* means pardon and absolution." (The Grosset Webster Dictionary) The gift of forgiveness is given us through the blood sacrifice of Christ Jesus. We cannot earn forgiveness of our sin, nor do we deserve it. Jesus paid the price for our forgiveness; the only way to be forgiven is through Him. God provided only one Way to be forgiven: through the sacrifice of His one and only begotten Son, Jesus Christ. All we can do is confess our sin, believe in Jesus, the One God sent, and accept this indescribable gift of forgiveness. This forgiveness is so complete that, once you accept it, your past, present, and future sins are all forgiven. It is hard for me to fathom how and why there are those who want to reject this gift.

While atonement for sin and forgiveness of sin came from Jesus' shed blood, it is the covering of the blood that allows the Spirit of God and our individual spirits to be reunited. In the Old Testament, the high priest spilled animal blood over the ark of the covenant once a year for the forgiveness of the Israelites' sins. The sacrificial blood flowed over the ark, covering it. This gives us a picture of the protection that the covering of the blood of Christ Jesus provides between our sinful nature and God's holiness.

Cover
(Relevant Scriptures: Exodus 12:7, 12–13; Psalms 32:1; Romans 4:7–8; Ephesians 1:13–14)

The definition of" *cover* is to conceal, shelter, protect and to clothe and envelop."(The Grosset Webster Dictionary) The sinless blood of Jesus provides the internal covering for the sinful nature within our souls, which enables the Holy Spirit to enter the soul area and fuse with an individual's spirit without coming into direct contact with the sinful nature within that person. Jesus' sinless, sacred blood is the robe of righteousness given to everyone who accepts Him as their Savior. This covering wraps His righteousness over the sinful nature and provides the protection needed for the Holy Spirit to enter the heart and fuse with a person's individual spirit. We are saved and reunited with the Spirit of God by the very righteousness of Christ Jesus.

Salvation does not come to us through our own righteousness; it is available only through the sinless, sacred covering of the blood of Jesus Christ. We didn't personally commit the sin that allowed the sinful nature to enter the soul of all humankind; rather, Adam and Eve rebelled, which gave rise to sin in humankind. In the same way, we do not personally pay the price for our salvation. Jesus paid for us by allowing His sacrificial blood to be shed. It is only through Him that we receive atonement for our sin and the covering of His righteousness.

Seal

"*Seal* means to place a seal on; validate. To fasten or close. To confirm and conclude. (The Grosset Webster Dictionary) Jesus' blood covering is the seal that finalizes God's plan of salvation. As Jesus took His final breath before He died on the cross, He yelled out, "It is finished!" Everything necessary to guarantee the salvation of humanity was accomplished that moment. All that is necessary for eternal salvation from that point on is for each individual to accept or reject what Jesus died to give us. How can Jesus guarantee our salvation if we accept him as our Savior? He does this in two ways. First, He saves us by His righteousness alone. Who or what can ever change the righteousness of Jesus? Second, the Holy Spirit enters our hearts and fuses with our individual spirits to guarantee our salvation in Christ. Our salvation in Christ is secured because the Holy Spirit is the keeper of our salvation.

Final Thoughts

(Relevant Scriptures regarding the attributes of humankind: Matthew 4:2, 27:48–56; Mark 4:38; John 11:35, 19:28. Relevant Scriptures regarding the attributes of God: Matthew 8:1–34, 9:1–8, 17:1–13; John 9:1–12, 11:38–44)

In Jesus, God the Father accomplished first in this one Man what He wanted to accomplish in all humanity: the reunion of Himself and humankind. Jesus, being God, had all the attributes of God. He raised Lazarus from the dead, proving that He had power over life and death. He defied the laws of nature when He commanded the raging sea to be quiet and walked on the water. He instantly healed the sick and made the blind see. He cast out demons, proving He had authority over the spiritual realm as well as the natural realm. Being all Man, He also had the same attributes of a human being. He wept, hungered, thirsted, slept, suffered, and died. Jesus' being fully God and completely Man gave him the responsibility for the sins of humankind and the authority that enabled Him to pay the price for sin. Like the first Adam, Jesus received His physical life by way of God's direct action and was born without the sinful nature in His soul. Unlike the first Adam, Jesus never rebelled against God and so the sinful nature was never able to enter His soul, making Him the spotless Lamb of God worthy to atone for the sins of the world.

Jesus also fulfilled the prophecies God spoke through the Old Testament prophets foretelling the coming of the Messiah. These prophecies were written centuries before Jesus was born and came through many different prophets. It would have been impossible to coordinate or manufacture the ways to fulfill all of the varied aspects spoken about the coming Messiah. Jesus fulfilled each and every one of them.

The Scriptures give an account of Jesus' transfiguration. One day, He took Peter, James, and John up a high mountain where there was no one else. Suddenly, Jesus was transfigured before their very eyes. His face shone like the sun and His clothes became as white as the light. Then, Moses and Elijah appeared before the four and talked with Jesus. While He was speaking, a bright cloud enveloped them all. A voice from the cloud said, "This is my son, whom I love; with him I am well pleased. Listen to him!" When the disciples heard this, they fell face down onto the ground. When they looked up, only Jesus was standing in front of them.

This has to be the most prestigious meeting in the history of the world. We have Moses, who represents the law, and Elijah, who represents the prophets of God. We have Jesus, who fulfills the law and the prophecies. Then, God the Father hides Himself in a cloud to protect the disciples from His glory, declares that Jesus is His very own Son, and instructs them to listen to His Son. Jesus is God's plan of salvation and the only Way to obtain forgiveness for sin and be reconciled with the Spirit of God. This is what is so very special about Jesus. Listen to Him.

CHAPTER 10

THE VEHICLE OF THE CROSS

(Relevant Scriptures: John 16:7; Matthew 26:36–75, 27:1–56; 2 Corinthians 5:21; John 15:13)

Writing this chapter brought back a memory I had long forgotten. It was at the very beginning of my mental and spiritual problems. My mind was full of confusion and horror, and I had no idea what to do. I was sitting at my kitchen table reading the Scriptures about Jesus' suffering and crucifixion. I had heard this story all my life, but on that day it touched my heart. I wept for the Lord and the awful suffering He endured to atone for sin. In that moment, for the first time, I realized the terrible price that He paid and saw the great love that was behind His sacrifice. It became even more compelling when I understood that Jesus had the power to stop His suffering any time He chose to do so.

It was a miracle that I came through the terrible battle of my soul unscathed and better than I had ever been.

I know for certain that the only reason I survived was because I sought the Lord Jesus with all my heart and mind. I believed He was the Savior of my soul and the only one who could help me out of my distress. My mind may have been in total disarray, but my belief in Jesus was the most solid and sane thing I had. What He did on the cross for the salvation of humanity is the greatest act of love this natural-realm world and the spiritual-realm world have ever known. At that single moment in history, He became the Savior of our souls.

For any plan to be successful, it must accomplish everything needed to come to completion and fulfill the purpose it was designed to serve. It was on the cross that Jesus completed the second phase of the plan of salvation and put it into action. In so doing, He made His sacrifice for the atonement of sin available to all who would believe in Him and accept Him as their Savior. Jesus is literally the Way for each individual to choose to be reunited with the Spirit of God.

There are three reasons why Jesus had to die in order to save humanity. One of the reasons I have already discussed. He had to satisfy the demands of the law, and to do that, He had to give a blood sacrifice. Jesus' death on the cross paid the price for sin and provided the covering for sin. However, it only made conditions right so that our individual spirits could reunite with the Spirit of God.

The second reason is that, until Jesus' death, the reunion between God and humanity had taken place only in Jesus. What had been accomplished in Jesus now had to be made available to all humankind. It was at the death of His body that His spirit was released to return to the spiritual realm. This opened the Way for the Holy Spirit to come and persuade us to accept Jesus as our Savior. The Holy Spirit woos us to Jesus so He can come into our soul and spirit, making reconciliation with God a reality in our lives. During the time between His resurrection and His return to the spiritual-realm kingdom, Jesus explained to His followers why He had to leave them. He said, "Unless I go away, the Counselor [Holy Spirit] will not come to you; but if I go, I will send him to you." (John 16: 7) Jesus is the Way for all who would accept Him to receive the Holy Spirit. It is the Holy Spirit who is the great gift of salvation, available only through Jesus' sacrifice.

There is a third reason why Jesus' death was necessary. Some question whether it was possible for Jesus' body to die a natural death. Death is the result of sin, and Jesus was completely without sin. His Spirit and His soul were at peace; because of this, He had perfect balance within His being, as did Adam and Eve before the fall. Sin could affect Him from the outside, but I am not sure that this would be enough to cause God's body to die. It is more likely that the death of Jesus' body would have to occur through the sin of others. Because of this, Jesus allowed himself to be led like a lamb to slaughter to the cross—on a mission to defeat humanity's great enemy, *death*. It was not the death of the body that He came to save us from, but the far greater spiritual death that occurred when we were separated from the Spirit of God. It was because of the sins of humanity that Jesus had to die, and it was through humankind's sinful actions that He was put to death on the cross.

I was taught that the sins of the whole world came upon Jesus as He hung on the cross. This thought always led me to question how that could be accomplished. It would mean that every sin ever committed by every human being descended upon Him at one time. To comprehend this, we have to understand more clearly the sinful nature harbored in our souls. Every sin that has ever been committed comes out of that sinful nature. God created us, and what He created in us is good. The sinful nature housed within us is of Satan and is foreign to our soul and spirit. When Jesus died for the sins of the entire world, He did so by taking Satan's sinful nature upon Himself. Since all sin, past, present, and future, comes from the sinful nature; every sin that has ever been or ever will be committed was atoned for by Jesus' singular sacrifice of His own life. When we accept Jesus as our Savior, every sin we have ever committed or ever will commit is already atoned for. When we accept Jesus, we activate that atonement—and the forgiveness for our own personal sins becomes a reality.

The big question is what took place as Jesus hung there on the cross? We know there was a terrible moment when He cried out, "My God, my God, why have you forsaken me?" (Matthew 27: 46) The part of Jesus that was fully

Man had never known a moment when He was not fully connected and at one with the Spirit of God, for He was God incarnate. The separation was horrifying for the human side of Jesus. I am sure it was the worst moment of His entire ordeal. I am also equally certain that it was the most agonizing moment for God the Father. It is one of the great mysteries of the Church that Jesus, who is God, could be separated from God. The only explanation that I can even begin to understand is that Jesus had both the spirit of Man and the Spirit of God fused together in the spirit area of His being. This alone would make Him all Man as well as completely God. It would mean that He inherited an individual human spirit from His mother and the Holy Spirit of God from His heavenly Father. If this is the case, then it is entirely possible that the two spirits separated before Jesus' body died.

The Spirit of God departed a split second before Satan's sinful nature came upon Jesus. In that moment, the sinful nature, which is the source of the sins of the entire world, came crashing down upon Jesus' body. In one agonizing flash of time, Jesus experienced two things He had never experienced before: separation from God the Father and the weight of sin. So, Jesus hung there alone as a sinless man, feeling forsaken by His heavenly Father and crushed by the weight of the sins of the world. The shock must have been unimaginable; He had never personally known the price of sin because He had never sinned. He had suffered at the hands of sinful people in a sinful world, but He did not have the sinful nature within Him, so He did not personally know the horror of it. Plus, He had never known the devastation of complete separation from God the Father.

Satan, in an attempt to destroy Jesus, brought his sinful nature down upon the Lord and tried to gain entrance into His soul. However, because Jesus was without sin, Satan's powerful sinful nature could not overcome Jesus' righteousness. Jesus endured the onslaught. When He had won, He proclaimed, "It is finished," and died. Why would God the Father leave Jesus at such a moment? The answer to that is really quite simple. It was humanity who had sinned, so only a human could pay the price for the sin. The apostle Paul explains it this way: "God made him [Jesus] who had no sin to be sin for us, so that in him we might become the righteousness of God." (2Corinthians 5:21) In other words, God the Father allowed this to happen to His very own Son so that sin could be defeated and all who would come to Jesus would be given Christ's righteousness. "Greater love has no one than this that he lay down his life for his friends." (John 15:13)What a friend we have in Jesus.

We are too often focused on the fact that Jesus is God that we do not always connect with the fact that He was also Man with the weaker human nature we all have. He could stand against every temptation to sin because He was God; nevertheless, He still had to contend with His own human nature. Jesus is all God and all Man, but it was the Man who was nailed to the cross. It was the Man who didn't back down from the cross. During Jesus' life in the body, God the Father had prepared His Son for this one horrifying event. Jesus was the only Way for God's plan of salvation to be accomplished. The human part of Jesus did not back down but won salvation for us all.

At Jesus' birth, the natural realm and spiritual realm came together to observe the birth of the living God. The magnitude of the event caused a magnificent star to form, announcing His birth and that the Light had come into the world. At Jesus' death, the world went dark and the dead walked on Earth. The curtain in the tabernacle that separated the Holy of Holies, where only the high priest could enter, tore open, thereby opening the Way for all of us to enter into the full presence of God.

The Transformation of the Cross
(Relevant Scriptures: Romans 8:1–17, 12:2; 2 Corinthians 3:18; Philippians 3:21)

One of the most profound and touching visions the Holy Spirit has ever given me came during the season of Lent. I was in prayer when I received a vision of three crosses on a distant hill. At first, it appeared as if the crosses were coming closer to me, but, in fact, my spirit was drawing nearer to them. As my spirit moved closer and closer, my complete focus was on the center cross where Jesus was being crucified. Then, much to my astonishment, I watched as my spirit entered into Christ's body, where I experienced the last moments of His life in the body. I could feel and hear His body struggling to breathe. From this experience, I would say that He died of suffocation. Although His body struggled with its natural instinct to draw breath, there was no struggle in His inner being, only a deadly silence and complete peace. My body felt it as He breathed His last breath and gave up His Spirit. The vision ended, and I sat pondering my privileged experience. I would never have imagined this on my own. When the memory of it comes to my mind, the old hymn "Were You There When They Crucified the Lord?" comes to mind, as well. Through some miracle of the spiritual realm I do not understand, I experienced the moment when Jesus died and gave His life for us all.

Few things are uglier than crucifixion. The practice of nailing a human body to a cross and watching as life slowly drains from it is offensive on many levels. The cross is the very symbol of all that is offensive about crucifixion, yet we wear crosses around our necks. Crosses adorn our church buildings and sanctuaries. We sing hymns such as "In the Cross of Christ I Glory," and we raise the cross as the symbol of the greatest love the world has known. What made the difference? How could such an instrument of torture turn into the symbol for love and forgiveness? It is simply because Jesus touched it. What He touches, He transforms and makes His own.

The cross is where Jesus substituted His life in the flesh for our life in the Spirit, changing forever the meaning of the cross. This instrument of death was transformed into a vehicle of life and became the symbol of God's great love for His people. There are some in the Church who would replace the cross as the symbol of Christianity because of the violence associated with it. While I imagine that these people mean well, I believe that they have missed the meaning of the cross as the vehicle of transformation. Those who are in Christ Jesus know that everything changed the day He died on the cross. Physical life turned to spiritual life, damnation to salvation, and condemnation to forgiveness. Law surrendered to grace, and separation from God was exchanged for everlasting life with God.

What a wonderful revelation it was when I came to know Jesus as the great transformer. One of the keys to a victorious Christian life is learning the ways of God so we may seek to submit to His way of doing things. To succeed in this, we must understand that God cannot undo certain events. The fall of humanity is certainly one such event. God could not turn back time and then proceed as if the fall had never happened. The consequences of the fall were already evident; it was done and could not be undone. He had to find another way to deal with the problem. The spoken word is another example of something that cannot be rescinded. Once words are spoken, whether for good or evil, they have an effect. If the words caused damage, then one must find a way to repair it. Sometimes, our troubles and heartaches come from our own actions; at other times, we feel pain through the sins of others. Then there is the pain and suffering that reaches us simply because we live in this violent world where sin, death, and disease are prevalent.

One of the things God has provided to heal our hurts and sorrows is the process of transformation. It is important to understand that transformation does not change the event; instead, it changes the repercussions. This is accomplished by changing the reactions to whatever has happened. The miracle of transformation is that it changes things in such a way to alter the harmful effects on our hearts and minds.

My first experience with transformation came from seeking release from the grief and sadness I experienced after my dad's death. I was so lonesome for him that I could not let go of my pain. All I really wanted was my dad back, but that was impossible, so I was trapped in a cycle of grief and pain. Nothing I tried seemed to work, so I sought the Lord for a way out of my dilemma. It was through the process of healing that I came to understand the miracle of God's gift of transformation. God touched each spot in my heart that had been damaged by grief and sadness until all the pain was gone. Memories of my dad came flooding back, but instead of bringing pain, they brought delight and joy. In one moment of revelation, God confirmed to me that my dad was safely in His care and our separation was only temporary. Peace flooded my soul and life took on the quality of eternity. The transformation of my dad's death was completed in me.

Over the years, I have become convinced that there is nothing God cannot transform if we are willing to do things His way. This truth has been proven to me over and over again. God took the dark days of horror and mental turmoil I endured and transformed my mind to light and health. I thank God for each day I live on His beautiful Earth. At the same time, I joyfully look forward to the moment when I close my eyes in death. There are moments when I can feel my spirit straining to be free of my body to fully enter the heavenly realm, where I will see Christ face-to-face. For me, He has transformed death to life, sadness to joy, fear to trust, and sickness to health. I face each day knowing that He will be there to supply all I need for whatever befalls me.

Jesus Is the Pivot Point of the Trinity
(Relevant Scriptures: Luke 24:49; John 14:5–21; Acts 4:12)

It was on the cross that Jesus became the central figure of the Godhead and the pivot point of the Trinity. In the book of John, as Jesus was preparing His disciples for His death, He made the following two statements: "I am the way, the truth and the life. No one comes to the Father except through me" (14:16) and "I will ask the Father and he will give you another Counselor [the Holy Spirit] to be with you forever—the Spirit of truth. The world cannot accept him, because it neither sees him nor knows him. But you know him, for he lives with you and will be in you" (14:16–17). These two statements emphasize what Jesus accomplished for us on the cross.

First, He atoned for the sins of all humankind and redeemed us from the death sentence required by the law (eternal separation from God). This gives us eternal, everlasting life with God the Father in His heavenly kingdom. For those who have accepted Jesus, their destiny is to go back to the Father and spend eternity in heaven with Him. They will return to their Creator as a redeemed, forgiven child of salvation. Jesus' second statement makes it clear that our life with God does not start when we die; it begins when we accept Him as our Savior. The world, or the unbeliever, cannot have the Holy Spirit inside because they have not accepted the covering for sin that is available only through Jesus' death. It is only with our sin covered that the Holy Spirit is able to dwell in our hearts (the deep mind of the soul area) and be diffused throughout our spirits. The moment we accept Jesus as our Savior is when we receive the Holy Spirit into our being. In that moment, we are instantly transformed from God's child of creation into His redeemed child of salvation.

Eternity with God begins when we accept Jesus as our Savior. When the Holy Spirit enters our being, we are spiritually alive in God and have the same resurrection power that Christ Jesus possesses. The kingdom of God literally comes to dwell within us, bringing with it God Himself and the potential to learn the principles of the spiritual realm while we still live in the natural realm. As we begin to grow spiritually in our knowledge of and relationship with the Holy Spirit, we become active citizens of both this natural-realm world and the spiritual-realm world. Beginning to learn the spiritual realm's principles has been the adventure of my life; it is like getting a head start on my eternal life in the spiritual realm. It is only through the life, death, and resurrection of Christ Jesus that our reconciliation with God is accomplished. Miss anything in life, but don't miss your salvation in Christ Jesus.

CHAPTER 11

PUTTING THE PLAN OF SALVATION INTO ACTION

(Relevant Scriptures: 1 Peter 3:18–19; John 20:10–18; Mark 16:1)

Jesus' death had a twofold effect. First, it provided the atonement for sin and the covering for the sinful nature, making it possible for the human spirit and God's Spirit to be reunited. Second, when the body of Jesus died, His Spirit was released to return to the spiritual realm. Up to this point, we have mainly sought to understand why Jesus is the Savior of the world and how He was able to pay the price for our sin. Now, we must look at the second effect of His death, which is the resurrection of His body and the release of His Spirit to return to the spiritual realm. It is through the death of His body that salvation is made possible, and it is through the release of His Spirit that salvation is put into operation.

It was at the very moment when Jesus died that the process began. What He had accomplished on the cross was now put into action. During the three days between His death and resurrection, Jesus activated the first step of the plan of salvation. He started this process in the spiritual realm with all those individuals who had lived on Earth and died before He died on the cross. When Jesus' Spirit left His body, He immediately went into the spiritual-realm area known as Paradise or the bosom of Abraham. This is where the spiritual citizens who had lived on Earth and died before the death and resurrection of Jesus resided, as they waited for the Savior. Jesus preached to those waiting spirits and offered them atonement for sin. He led everyone who believed Him and chose to accept His salvation to the gated area of the spiritual realm, where they would live forever in the full presence of God the Father. At that moment, salvation became a reality in the spiritual-realm world.

On the third day after Jesus' death, the resurrection of His body was complete and He left the grave behind. Mary Magdalene was the first to see the resurrected Jesus. She had come to the grave to prepare His lifeless body for final burial, but she found an empty grave, where she sat crying in despair. Jesus appeared before her, proving that He was alive and had risen from the grave. He comforted her and gave her a special mission to go tell the other disciples that He had risen.

The significance of this is enormous for two reasons. It was not by chance that Jesus made his first appearance to a woman. It had been a woman who was first deceived by Satan, resulting in sin and death for all humankind. It was through the womb of a woman that the Son of God was born to be the Savior of the world. This Savior born of a woman had now gained victory over sin and death, opening the Way for all to be saved. So, Jesus gave the honor to a woman to proclaim that He was alive and had conquered sin and death. In so doing, He completed the final transformation of the shame that womanhood had been under ever since Eve ate the forbidden fruit. He freed Mary Magdalene and all other women to throw off that shame and walk in the full authority that was given to them at the time of creation. This was Jesus' very first act of forgiveness and transformation on Earth after His resurrection.

The mission He gave to Mary Magdalene had another important meaning. Mary had come to the grave that morning to anoint the dead body of Jesus for final burial, as was the Jewish tradition. She completed that mission in a way she never dreamed she would. The Church is called the body of Christ. This is because the Spirit of God was fully housed in Jesus' human body. When His body died, His Spirit was released to live in all those who accepted Him as their Savior. So, anyone who accepts Jesus as his or her Savior has the Holy Spirit housed in his or her body and is part of His church, which is called the body of Christ. Mary Magdalene went that morning to prepare the body of Christ Jesus—and prepare the body of Christ (His Church) is exactly what she did. She prepared the waiting believers to receive their risen Lord.

A Time of Transition
(Relevant Scripture: John 20:19–22)

This encounter with Mary began a forty-day time of transition when Jesus walked on Earth and spent time with His disciples. These were the men and women who were going to be the first to preach the gospel of Christ. He needed to prove to them that He had indeed risen from the dead and was truly the Savior of the world. He also needed to heal the damage that had been done to their faith through the events leading up to the crucifixion. However, His most important mission during this time was to prepare His followers for the coming of the Holy Spirit. Their lives were going to dramatically change in ways they never dreamed possible.

The coming of the Holy Spirit would change the interaction between Jesus and His followers. No longer would He appear in the natural/physical realm of visible matter, but in the unseen world of the spiritual realm. The Holy Spirit was going to be able to dwell within people's soul and spirit areas. In other words, the reunion between the Spirit of God and the disciples' individual human spirits was going to become a reality. This was not the only major change the disciples were going to have to adapt to. Until now, they had sought to please God by obeying His law. However, the law was only temporary, as Jesus' sacrifice meant the end of Mosaic Law. Righteousness, or rightness with God, was now obtained only through faith in Jesus. God had promised in the Old Testament that one day He would write His laws on our hearts. It is through the Holy Spirit in the heart area of our souls that this promise is fulfilled. The biggest change was that the Holy Spirit, who is the gift of salvation, could be obtained only by faith, through the act of believing in and accepting Jesus.

These forty days between Jesus' resurrection and ascension into heaven mark some of the most intimate moments between Jesus and His followers. For the disciples, it was a time of great joy and excitement as well as confusion. Jesus was among them, yet it was not quite the same way as before His death. He was the same, yet He had changed. Before His death and resurrection, He walked and lived with them. However, now He appeared among them. They would be clustered behind locked doors when, suddenly, Jesus would appear in their midst. Simply put, He was no longer confined by the laws of the natural-realm world. This must have been an especially sweet time for the Lord. I believe that He had a great deal of fun popping in on those who knew Him best. His suffering was over, His mission was accomplished, and He was proving His victory to those men and women who would be at the forefront of building His Church.

One special moment when Jesus appeared to the disciples as they gathered behind a locked door is especially meaningful. They were overjoyed to see Him as Jesus spoke words of peace, calming their fears. He made the connection between God the Father and Himself by saying, "As the Father has sent me [into the world], I am sending you [into the world]." (John 20:21) God the Father had sent His Son, the very fullness of God embodied in the flesh, into the world to save it. Jesus was now sending His followers into the world so they could carry the message of salvation. In this way, they would lead others to believe and accept Jesus. Jesus then breathed on them and said, "Receive the Holy Spirit." (John 20:22) He did this so they would have the very Spirit of God dwelling within them, empowering them to take the message of salvation out into the world. This special happening shows that Jesus is the giver of the Holy Spirit and that it is through Him that we receive the Spirit of God inside ourselves.

After Jesus' Ascension
(Relevant Scriptures: John 16:7; Acts 1:4–5; Romans 8:9; Acts 2:1–41)

Jesus had prepared His followers for His ascension into heaven. They were to wait in Jerusalem for the gift that God the Father had promised them and about which

Jesus had spoken. During the time leading up to His death, Jesus told His disciples, "It is for your good that I am going away. Unless I go away, the Counselor [Holy Spirit] will not come to you: but if I go, I will send Him to you." (John 16:7)He told them, "John baptized with water, but in a few days you will be baptized in the Holy Spirit." (Acts 1:5)The Holy Spirit is the great gift of salvation that God the Father had promised to all who believe in His Son. For it is written, "If anyone does not have the Spirit of Christ, he does not belong to Christ." (Romans 8:9)

When Jesus was taken up into heaven, He was seated at the right hand of God the Father. The Holy Spirit was released on Earth in a new and powerful way. He had always been on Earth, but now His mission had changed. Before Jesus accomplished atonement for sin, the Holy Spirit could interact with people only from outside their bodies. He could come upon them, but He could not dwell within them. This is still true until an individual believes in and accepts the sacrifice of Jesus. It is only then that the Holy Spirit can come into the believer's heart and spirit and permanently dwell there.

When the day of Pentecost arrived, the believers were all together in one house. Suddenly, a sound like that of a violent wind came from heaven and filled the whole place. They saw a fire that separated and rested on each of them, and they were all filled with the Holy Spirit. The change was immediate. They had a new and deeper connection with God. They were empowered with the truth of the knowledge of Christ Jesus. Their relationship with God was deeper and more intimate and affected both the conscious areas of their souls and their spirits. Now, they had the very Spirit of God within them, giving them the power to know Him and to bring others to know Him, as well. At that moment, they began to speak in languages they did not know. It was such an event that a crowd had heard the wind and come to see what had happened. They heard the disciples speaking in languages familiar to them and saw with their own eyes this amazing event. Peter, for the first time, stood up and started preaching under the anointing of the Holy Spirit. On that day, three thousand people became believers and were baptized in the Holy Spirit. The Church was born and salvation in Christ Jesus became a reality on Earth.

It was on the day of Pentecost that the Holy Spirit became available to all who would accept Jesus as their Savior. It is through the Holy Spirit that Christians are forever connected to God the Father, and it is only through the sacrifice of Jesus Christ, His Son, that we can receive the Holy Spirit. The ultimate goal of everything Jesus did was to enable the Holy Spirit and our individual spirits to come together again. If not for the coming of the Holy Spirit, the work of salvation would have remained inactive and the goal of salvation would have failed. These things are what Jesus came to accomplish. He died to give them to us.

The Process of Believing
(Relevant Scripture: Romans 10:8–17)

God's plan of salvation overcame every obstacle that stood in the way of the reunion of God and humankind, with one exception. There is one major obstacle that God cannot overcome without our cooperation. He cannot simply bestow salvation in individuals or masses of people. Instead, each individual has to accept it. The final step of salvation is accomplished only through humankind's free will, with each person making the choice to accept or reject what Jesus did on the cross. The problem became this: how to provide a way for each individual to make that choice.

The apostle Paul teaches in the book of Romans that "everyone who calls on the name of the Lord [Jesus] will be saved." He goes on to explain, "How, then, can they call on the one they have not believed in? And how can they believe in the one whom they have not heard? And how can they hear without someone preaching to them? And how can they preach unless they are sent?" (Romans 10: 14-15) On the day of Pentecost, these questions were answered. The Holy Spirit came to the first believers and dwelled within them, empowering them to preach and teach about salvation through Jesus, the Christ. They were to proclaim salvation and open the Way for all who believed and called upon Jesus to receive eternal salvation and be forever united with God the Father, God the Son, and God the Holy Spirit. This is the way in which the gospel of Christ was first set in motion, and it is the way it is accomplished to this very day.

The ability to believe begins through the process of hearing. The ability to believe that Jesus is the Savior of the world comes from hearing the truth about Jesus through preaching. When we hear any truth spoken, it is a powerful thing, but when we hear the truth about Jesus being spoken, it is anointed by the Holy Spirit and is the most powerful message of truth we can ever hear. The Holy Spirit is the one who anoints and quickens the truth of the gospel of Christ. So, when we reject the spoken or written Word of God, we are rejecting the work of the Holy Spirit, which is to bring us to believe in Jesus and bring to fruition the plan of salvation.

As I said earlier, it is with our spirits that we can know God—and deep within every spirit is the memory of when it was in God's presence. It is this deep spiritual desire to be reunited with God that keeps our spirits constantly looking for God until we finally find Him in Christ Jesus. The process of coming to believe in Jesus goes something like this: We hear the Holy Spirit–anointed gospel of Christ preached, and it enters the conscious areas of our minds. We think about what we have heard and ponder its meaning, deciding whether we believe it or not. This part of the process may go on for some time, but, eventually, the truth of Christ begins to filter down into our deep mind (the heart area of the soul) and the heart begins to communicate the message to the spirit. The human spirit has been searching for the truth. When it hears it, it begins to communicate to the deep mind (the heart), "This is it! This is truth! This is the way back to union with God!" Once this message from our spirit enters the heart area, the heart begins to believe. Then, the message is filtered back into the conscious area of the mind and confirms that what we have heard about Jesus is the truth—and we believe.

The apostle Paul writes, "For it is with your heart you believe and are justified, and it is with your mouth that you confess and are saved." (Romans 10:10) This tells us that the act of believing in salvation is not a matter for the conscious mind alone. With our hearts, we must believe that Jesus is our Savior. This is accomplished through the Holy Spirit's anointing of the gospel of Christ, which filters through the heart (deep mind) and into the spirit, which enables the heart to believe. When the individual spirit recognizes the Holy Spirit's anointing, it confirms the truth to the heart. In other words, God's Spirit confirms to the human spirit the truth of salvation through Jesus. This is when we believe the truth of salvation in Christ Jesus and accept Him as our Savior. Then, we confess with our mouths what we believe. It is in hearing our own confession of faith in Christ Jesus that we confirm to our conscious minds, our hearts, and our spirits that we believe that He has saved us.

Salvation is a gift that must be either accepted or rejected. It is not possible to accept the gift of salvation unless we believe in our hearts that Jesus is Lord and that God raised Him from the dead once He atoned for our sins. Why would anyone ask Jesus to be his or her Savior while not believing that He is the Savior? The only way to accept Jesus' sacrifice is through the process of believing. To *believe* means to put credence in; have confidence in.(The Grosset Webster Dictionary) These words, to trust, have faith in, be certain of, and rely on are also related to the act of believing. In this natural-realm world, we seek to understand before we believe; however, in the realm of the spirit, the act of believing is opposite. It is through the act of believing that we come to know and understand what we believe. Two of my favorite quotes of Saint Augustine are true. He said, "Seek not to understand that you may believe, but believe that you may understand" and "Faith is to believe what you do not see, the reward of this faith is to see what you believe." (BrainyQuote Website)

It is often said that the existence of God and the truth of salvation cannot be proven. This may be so if one attempts to prove these things through natural-realm reasoning and the five senses. The problem is that salvation is a spiritual happening and is realized through spiritual-realm principles that are filtered through our natural reasoning. The existence of God and the truth of salvation are easily proven through the process of believing. Proof of the existence of God and salvation through Jesus is given over and over again to each individual who believes in Him. One of the great surprises in my walk with the Lord is His willingness to prove Himself to me. All we need to do is seek Him with our whole hearts and believe. The understanding will eventually follow.

God's Magnificent Plan

What Happens When We Accept Jesus?
(Relevant Scriptures: John 3:1–8; 1 Corinthians 6:17; 2 Thessalonians 2:13; 1 Peter 1:2)

The Holy Spirit is the gift that God the Father promised to all who would believe in His Son, Jesus. It is through the Holy Spirit that we are born again of the Spirit of God. The process of being born again has always been a mystery. It was in the dark of night when a Pharisee (a Jewish religious leader) named Nicodemus came to visit Jesus, seeking to understand what it meant to be born again. He had heard Jesus preaching that to see the kingdom of God; a person must be born again. Nicodemus could not figure out how a grown man could be born again, as he certainly could not enter his mother's womb a second time. Jesus answered, "I tell you the truth, no one can enter the kingdom of God unless he is born of water and the Spirit. Flesh gives birth to flesh and Spirit gives birth to spirit." (John 3:5-6) The first birth is when one is born in the flesh through the mother's birth canal. This birth is one of water. It is when a woman's water breaks that the human baby is ready to be born. The second birth is spiritual and takes place when we are born again of the Spirit of God. In other words, when a baby comes into this world and is alive in the flesh, it does not have the Spirit of God living within it. This is the reason why babies come to Earth, to make the choice to be born again in the Spirit. We are born spiritually dead to God, but when we accept Jesus as our Savior, our spirit is reunited with the Holy Spirit and we are once again spiritually alive and connected to God.

The Process of Being Born Again
(Relevant Scriptures: Galatians 5:24; Colossians 2:9–15; Romans 2:28–29)

The process of being born again begins when we believe that Jesus is the Savior of the world. We accept His atonement and forgiveness for our sin. It is at this moment that, figuratively speaking, His sacrificial blood enters our souls and covers the sinful nature housed deep in our hearts. This is reminiscent of how the high priests in the Old Testament spilled the blood of sacrificial animals over the ark of the covenant. This covering of our sinful nature is the robe of Christ's righteousness, which is necessary for the Holy Spirit to enter the heart area deep within the soul. It is then that the Holy Spirit performs a supernatural surgery called circumcision of the heart. This is when the sinful nature attached to a person's heart is severed or cut away from the heart area of the soul. At this point, the sinful nature loses its life supply and begins to shrivel and die. The sinful nature's dying process is a slow one that does not end until the body dies. The miracle of this is that the sinful nature cannot follow one into the spiritual realm because it is then destined to die along with the flesh. Once this has occurred, the Holy Spirit enters the area of the individual spirit and is diffused through that spirit. At that moment, we are born again of the Spirit of God and the purpose for Jesus' sacrifice is fulfilled. We are reunited with God and are destined for all eternity to live in His full presence in his heavenly kingdom.

Children of Creation and Children of Salvation
(Relevant Scriptures: Romans 8:16–17; Acts 2:38–39)

We are all God's children of creation. He loves us equally. However, when we are born again of God's Spirit, we also become His children of salvation. This is when we start a new spiritual life in relationship with the Holy Spirit of God. As is the case with every newborn life, we begin to grow in our knowledge of and relationship with God. Some of us are immediately aware of our spiritual rebirth, while others have little or no awareness that this miracle took place in them. Varying conditions can affect one's consciousness of God's presence within. The differences may be a result of the ways in which we have been taught, of different personalities perceiving things differently, how old we are, and what we are called to do in God's kingdom, Some of us come to the Lord with damaged souls, while others are simply quiet believers. God can come upon us like a strong wind or a barely discernible whisper of a breeze. This has nothing to do with favoritism, for God loves us equally and with great passion. The important thing isn't how the Holy Spirit comes to dwell in your heart; the most important thing is that He is there and you are His born-again child of salvation. If you believe in your heart that Jesus is Lord, have asked Him to be your Savior, and have confessed with your mouth that you believe in Him, then you are His born-again child of salvation whom He will never leave or forsake.

I do not recall exactly when I accepted the Lord as my Savior. I do believe that it was long before my dad died and sometime in my childhood, for I cannot remember a time when I did not believe in Jesus. However, I had little awareness of His presence until I sought Him with all my heart during the time when I experienced mental turmoil. I don't know why this is so. In the church I attended, it was a requirement that I be interviewed by a church elder before I was confirmed. The elder asked me, "What does Jesus mean to you?" The answer I gave was immediate and without forethought. It shocked both the elder and me.

I said, "He is my very life." With that statement, my interview was over. I was flabbergasted by my answer because, at the time, my faith in and relationship with Jesus was not nearly at that level. It was not until I was in my thirties that this memory came back to me. I realized that what I had said at that moment was prophetic, as it exactly described what Jesus became to me. "He is my very life." That is what He is to all of us because our spiritual life in God depends on Him.

Section Three

THE CERTAINTY OF SALVATION

CHAPTER 12

THE CERTAINTY OF SALVATION

(Relevant Scripture: John 10:28)

In the first section of this book, we concentrated on the conditions that caused the need for salvation of human souls and the obstacles that God had to overcome to provide a way for our salvation. The second section focused on how God overcame the obstacles. Then, it centered on Jesus, who is the actual Way of salvation. The main focus of this last section is the certainty of the salvation we have in Christ Jesus. It is my firm belief that the Lord desires that each of His children of salvation live in humble confidence of His loving care. He desires that we be assured of our eternal destination in His heavenly kingdom, where we will live forever in His presence. Jesus makes this statement about those who follow Him: "I give them eternal life, and they shall never perish; no one can snatch them out of my hand" (John 10:28).

In my personal quest to live in the knowledge that my salvation is secured for all eternity, I found that my heart and mind would not totally accept this truth on the foundation of one or two Scriptures. I had to mature spiritually, grow in my understanding of God's plan of salvation, and know in my inner being how it works in order to fully accept the assurance of my eternal destination in Christ. Satan has attacked me many times on this subject, and every time, by the power of the Lord, I have won the battle and come out with an ever-deepening conviction of the certainty of salvation for those who have accepted Jesus. To continue to grow our faith in this area, we must first deepen our understanding of the Holy Spirit and His role in the plan of salvation.

The Holy Spirit
(Relevant Scriptures: John 7:37–39, 14:26, 16:5–16; Matthew 28:19; 1 Corinthians 2:10–12, 3:16, 6:11; 1 John 5:18; Titus 3:5; Romans 8:27)

The Holy Spirit is the invisible presence of God in the world. He is as essential to our spiritual life in God as the air we breathe is to our physical life. At the time of creation, God the Father breathed into Adam's nostrils the breath of physical life. Then, after the resurrection, Jesus, the Son, breathed upon the disciples while saying to them, "Receive the Holy Spirit." In so doing, Jesus imparted the breath of His spiritual life to His followers. Shortly after this event, on the day of Pentecost, the Holy Spirit descended on the waiting believers in Jesus, entered their hearts, and was fused with their individual spirits. This process continues to this day for all who believe in their hearts and accept Jesus as their Savior. In the same way God the Father gave us life in the flesh, Jesus gave us His spiritual life though the Holy Spirit.

The Holy Spirit is God. He is eternal, all-powerful, all-knowing, and omnipresent. He is the third person of the Trinity, equal in every way to the Father and to Jesus, the Son. In the beginning, God the Father spoke the commands that brought forth the creation of this natural world. However, it was the power of the Holy Spirit that hovered over the face of the deep which brought forth the life that God the Father called into existence. It is the same with salvation. Jesus came to Earth to provide the Way and conditions for the salvation of humankind. This was His work and His mission, but it is the Holy Spirit who carries out Christ's work and completes the process of salvation in the believer. Whereas Jesus is the Way of salvation, the Holy Spirit is the power and protector of the salvation Jesus provides. For all those who have accepted Jesus as their Savior, the function of the Holy Spirit is like a protector or keeper. He is the keeper of our soul. He protects the work of Christ in the believer. It is the Holy Spirit that keeps the believer spiritually safe, allowing nothing to take away a person's salvation.

The Holy Spirit used an event in my own life to give me deeper understanding about His role as preserver and protector of salvation. I needed major surgery on my spine because the main nerve to my left arm was badly pinched and dying. The surgeon took bone from my hip and placed it in the neck area of my spine to relieve the pressure on the nerve. After the surgery, I had to wear a neck brace (collar) day and night until the bone had fused together. I hated wearing that collar, so I prayed to the Lord, asking Him to help me love it. To this day, the collar sits in my scarf drawer. I cannot bear to throw it away because of what it represents.

I received the revelation that the collar represented the work of the Holy Spirit in my life. What the surgeon did to my spine to save my arm represented the work of salvation that Jesus did for me. After the surgery, the surgeon placed the collar around my neck to protect his work. Without that collar, one sudden movement, such as a fall, could have permanently undone the surgeon's repair. The Holy Spirit is the collar for every saved individual. He protects salvation in Christ from harm. As protector and keeper of salvation, He will not allow Christ's work to be undone in any believer. It is His mission and His work to keep us safely secured in Christ Jesus. Our flesh may fail us, but the Holy Spirit will never fail us. After receiving this revelation, my heart soared and assurance of my salvation began to take root in my heart.

A Seed and a Seal and an Inheritance

(Relevant Scriptures: 1 Peter 1:3–5, 23; Ephesians 1:13–14; 2 Corinthians 1:21–22; Hebrews 9:15–16; Romans 8:15–17, 8:38–39)

When we are born again of the Spirit of God, we are born of imperishable seed. "For you have been born again, not of perishable seed, but of imperishable" (1 Peter 1:23) A seed is the basis of new life, growth, and fruitfulness. An imperishable seed also has within it eternal, everlasting, immortal, indestructible, permanent life. It cannot be destroyed and cannot die, because the seed holds the life of God, made available to us through the death of Jesus. Jesus prepared His disciples for His death with this statement: "I tell you the truth, unless a kernel of wheat falls to the ground and dies, it remains only a single seed. But if it dies, it produces many seeds" (John 12:24). Jesus is the imperishable seed, and it was through Jesus' death that the Holy Spirit was released to dwell within people's hearts and spirits. Once we are born again of God's Spirit, we have His permanent and everlasting life within our souls, fused with our individual spirits. This cannot be undone.

As believers, not only are we born again of God's Spirit, but we are also sealed in the Holy Spirit as a guarantee of our salvation in Jesus. Our final destination is secured for all eternity. Paul writes, "Now it is God who makes both us and you stand firm in Christ. He anointed us, set his seal of ownership on us and put his Spirit in our hearts as a deposit, guaranteeing what is to come" (2 Corinthians

1:21–22). This deposit is the guarantee that everything we inherit through Christ Jesus will be ours in full. It is the Holy Spirit who guarantees this because He is the one who causes us to stand firm in Christ and guards our salvation until we receive our full inheritance as God's children of salvation. This is the inheritance one receives when one becomes a child of salvation. The inheritance became available to all who accept that Jesus died on the cross on our behalf. An inheritance is not dependent on what the recipient does; instead, it is based on who the recipient is in relation to the one bestowing the inheritance. Jesus was predestined to be the Savior of the world before the world was created. Those who accept Jesus as their Savior are destined to spend all eternity in the presence of God in His heavenly kingdom.

Salvation in Christ Jesus is not a weak thing. As the above Scripture says, through Jesus' sacrifice, God the Father anoints us, sets His seal of ownership on us, and gives us the Holy Spirit, guaranteeing our full inheritance in His heavenly kingdom. The certainty of our salvation is confirmed by God the Father, God the Son, and God the Holy Spirit. There is nothing stronger or more certain in this natural-realm world or in the spiritual-realm world than the salvation of all those who accept Jesus as their Savior. Salvation was designed to be a permanent solution to a spiritual-realm problem. It is accomplished when God allows all spiritual-realm citizens who were affected by Lucifer's and humanity's fall to decide whom they believe and whom they will follow. God's heavenly kingdom will be filled by those who have chosen to be there through their belief in Jesus and acceptance of Him as their Savior.

Just as the Father, Son, and Holy Spirit guarantee the certainty of our salvation, our conscious minds, hearts, and individual spirits confirm and solidify the decision to accept Jesus as Savior. In other words, the decision to accept Jesus as Savior is not a choice our conscious minds make only to change on a whim or because of a different mood or idea. We must always remember that salvation is not complete until we believe in our heart. The combined belief of the conscious mind and the heart of man (the deep mind) form the control center of our being, and our own individual spirits validate the truth of salvation in Christ Jesus. Once you believe in your heart, your heart knows the truth, and then the truth is confirmed to your conscious mind. You have just made an irrevocable decision and are born again of the Spirit of God. Through the believers' own free will, they have chosen to believe God and have enlisted Jesus as the Savior of their souls. Now, salvation is dependent on Him and under His control. You are His child of salvation and are again spiritually alive in Him. You have been born of His Spirit and cannot change that any more than you can change the fact that you were born in the flesh when you entered this world. Nothing can ever change it because the Holy Spirit protects your salvation.

CHAPTER 13

EVERYTHING CHANGES

(Relevant Scriptures: 2 Corinthians 5:17; Galatians 3:21–25, 4:6–7, 6:11–16; Hebrews 8:1–13, 9:15; James 2:10)

When we accept Christ Jesus as our Savior, we are forever joined in Him. The apostle Paul writes, "Therefore, if anyone is in Christ, he is a new creation; the old has gone, and the new has come" (2 Corinthians 5:17). At the moment when we are reunited with God through Christ Jesus, everything changes. We go from spiritual death to spiritual life, from separation from God to reunion with God, and we are transformed from God's child of creation into God's redeemed child of salvation. We are an entirely new creation and live under a new covenant. We go from living under the old covenant of the law to living under the new covenant of grace. Change of any kind can throw us off balance, but change this radical can cause us difficulty in making the adjustment.

From the moment we are born into this world, the sinful nature is within us. We live with the knowledge of good and evil and the condemnation that accompanies the law. We are accustomed to this system because it is all we know. However, when we begin our new life in Christ, we live under the new covenant of grace and begin the process of learning to walk in the Spirit. This is an enormous transition—from trying to be good by following a list of rules to actually becoming good through a change of heart, through the Holy Spirit's ministry within us. The old covenant of the law and the new covenant of grace are so very different that it is helpful to contrast them.

The old covenant of the law focuses on what self does. The law governs by external rules and focuses on what we do. It brings with it a curse because it demands obedience to the whole law. Under the law, we serve as slaves. The effect is bondage. By contrast, the new covenant of grace focuses on what Christ Jesus has already done. The work of Christ in us causes change from within through the blessing of the Holy Spirit. Grace says to believe in Jesus and live. Under the new covenant of grace, we serve as a son (a child of God). The effect of this is freedom to follow the Holy Spirit within us. When we compare these two covenants, it is clear that they are opposites. Scripture informs us that the new covenant of grace is overwhelmingly superior to the old covenant of the law.

The Law
(Relevant Scripture: Exodus 20)

Scripture also makes the radical statement that "Christ is the end of the law." (Romans 10:4) This is hard for us to comprehend because we know that the law is perfect and right, the standard of righteousness. The problem with obtaining righteousness by obeying the law is not because the law isn't perfect. The problem is that we have the sinful nature within us; obeying the law can do nothing to change that fact. To make matters worse, the law actually agitates the sinful nature, causing it to want to rebel and be even more sinful. The law has no power to make us righteous because we cannot perfectly obey the law. In other words, the problem is the sinful nature within us, not the standard of the law. The law has no power to destroy the sinful nature. Every sinful act we commit comes out of that nature. Humanity's sinful nature is the problem that keeps us separated from God's presence, rendering the law completely impotent as an instrument of salvation.

During Jesus' time on Earth, He delivered His teachings to those people who lived under the law. In so doing, He was preparing them for the coming covenant of grace by showing them the futility of trying to achieve personal righteousness by obeying the law. Jesus directed his strongest words about the law at the Pharisees. The Pharisees were the most ardent and phony keepers of the law. Jesus called them vipers. These men were masters at watering down God's pure righteousness. They piled on more and more rules for the people to follow, turning God's commandments into something that people could actually attempt to follow. The Pharisees were full of pride and self-righteousness, two sins that are always present within keepers of the law. The biggest danger of having pride and self-righteousness is that they create a false sense of personal rightness and keep people from seeking the true righteousness of God.

It was during the Sermon on the Mount when Jesus spoke some powerful words about the law. In this sermon, Jesus spoke of the external possibility of keeping the law and then unveiled the internal impossibility (for human beings) of perfectly keeping the law. He used two of the Ten Commandments to illustrate His point. Jesus said, "You have heard that it was said to the people long ago, 'Do not murder, and anyone who murders will be subject to judgment.' But I tell you that anyone who is angry at his brother will be subject to judgment" (Matthew 5:21–22). "You have heard that it was said, 'Do not commit adultery.' But I tell you that anyone who looks at a woman lustfully has already committed adultery with her in his heart" (Matthew 5:27–28). One might be able to avoid committing an act of murder, but it is impossible for anyone never to be angry at another person. We may never physically commit the act of adultery; however, never looking upon another lustfully is an entirely different matter. Jesus took these external controls and exposed their inability to affect the internal sinfulness of humankind. In this way, Jesus was showing people that they were helpless to defeat their sinful nature. It is from this helpless position that we must seek the only Way open for humanity to be freed from the slavery of sin.

The Hopelessness of Trying to Be Saved by Way of the Law

During a family gathering some years ago, the conversation turned to the subject of salvation. A dear friend of our family said, "I know there is a line between the saved and unsaved, but I just don't know exactly where that line is." As much as some people fight against it, the truth remains that Jesus is the line. All who have accepted His gift of salvation being born of the Spirit of God are saved. There is no other measure of salvation. Our friend was having trouble understanding where the line of salvation was drawn because he was using the measure from the Tree of the Knowledge of Good and Evil. He was looking for the good in humankind to somehow cancel out the sin in humankind, which simply isn't possible. The good in us will never be able to rid us of the sinful nature harbored in our souls. This is true no matter how sincerely we may desire it not to be. Our friend was simply using the wrong measure. Using the measure of good and bad behavior to determine who is saved is ineffective. It is as futile as giving someone an empty gallon jug along with the instructions to use it as the only rule of measure to determine how far the Earth is from the moon. It would be impossible, for that instrument was never meant to measure distance.

If we think it through for a minute, we can see why this is so. If the good we do cancels out the bad we do, then the measure is uneven. Let's say that you have committed a couple more sins than I have committed. Do I go to heaven and you don't? Perhaps your sinful acts are not quite as bad as my sinful acts. Is it reasonable to think that you should be allowed one or two more sins to make things fair? How can we ever judge fairly? But even if we could, it would do nothing to eliminate the sinful nature that is in us. Because sin lives in us, God cannot live in us. We can try to make the choice to follow God's commandments and eliminate some of the consequences of sin, but we cannot rid ourselves of the sinful nature from within our hearts. We are fallen spiritual-realm children of creation who have the sinful nature in our souls. Any good we do can never change this.

The Purpose of the Law
(Relevant Scriptures: Romans 3:19–24, 7:7–13)

While God did not give us the law so that our souls could be saved, He did give it for important and specific purposes. My first understanding of the Ten Commandments was that God made a list of rules and demanded we follow them to live in obedience to Him. When we broke those rules, failing to comply with His commandments, He punished us for disobeying. Today, I realize that my understanding was completely out of line with the truth. The consequences of breaking the law were already present and operating long before God gave us the Ten Commandments. What God did when He handed down the law was reveal the standard to which humankind was already subject. He gave us the Ten Commandments as a compass indicating what to do and what not to do so that we might avoid the consequences that always follow breaking them. To the same extent that we are able to follow the law, we are able to avoid suffering some of the consequences of breaking the law. My mother once said, "The Ten Commandments were never meant to save you; God gave them to humankind to help us have a happy life." It is true that obeying the Ten Commandments can indeed help us avoid many pitfalls and give us a happier life.

A Corral

The first function of the law was to operate as a corral, restraining humankind from totally yielding to the sinful nature. When God gave Moses the Ten Commandments, He had already been striving with His fallen children for a long time. It is difficult for us to comprehend how deeply humankind had fallen into depravity and how little they knew of God's true nature and will. Humankind was following the desires of the sinful nature with complete abandon and refused to follow God. Long before giving us the Ten Commandments, God had destroyed most all of humankind, sparing only the godly family of Noah. He did this in hopes of raising a less depraved people who would follow Him. However, the people who came after the great flood also followed the sinful nature and began worshiping gods of their own making. This led to more suffering and depravity. From this climate of human chaos, God chose a people to teach how to control the behavior that emerges from the sinful nature. Through giving the Ten Commandments to Moses, God gave us all a temporary tool that taught us how to restrain our sinful behavior until He gave a permanent solution for sin.

A Mirror

At times, I have found myself in situations best described by the adage "I can't see the forest for the trees." When we perceive a problem and yet are unable to see its source, any hope of finding a solution is diminished. God faced this kind of dilemma with His fallen children. They were blind to their God, lost in a forest of sin, suffering under the consequences of that sin, and unable to find a solution. The second function of the law was to be the mirror reflecting the standard of righteousness. This two-way mirror illuminated the righteousness of God and, at the same time, exposed the unrighteousness of humankind. It is through this mirror that we can clearly see the standard by which we will be measured, for it is God's righteousness that we must live up to, not the letter of the law. The law, a representation of God's nature, is the permanent standard of right and wrong behavior. However, it is not a vessel to bring God's Spirit back to oneness with humanity.

God gave us the law as a means of controlling the sinful nature from the outside. At the time He gave us the Ten Commandments; God was only able to use external control to influence people's behavior. The law is the foundation on which all civil society rests. It gives us the parameters of right behavior. It was meant to be a temporary means of protection from the awful consequences of sin.

The Covenant of Grace

(Relevant Scriptures: Romans 8:1–11; 10:4; Luke 15:11–24; 2 Corinthians 3:1–18; Ephesians 2:4–8)

The need to save humankind has never been primarily about human behavior. It has always been about dealing with the sinful nature and the damage it does to our souls and spirits. This damage was first inflicted by Lucifer's fall in the spiritual realm and next by Adam and Eve's fall in the natural-realm world. The sinful nature within us must be dealt with before we may be born again of the Spirit of God. Once the Holy Spirit has entered a person's soul and spirit, He is able to cut the life supply of the sinful nature lodged in the heart. This makes the sinful nature lose power and eventually die with our flesh. The source of sinful behavior within us is in the process of dying, and we are, simultaneously, in the process of being freed from sin. It is by God's grace that we die and are freed from the sinful nature within us.

God created this world in an act of grace. Also by His grace, He sent His Son to atone for our sin. And it is through grace that the Holy Spirit's ministry seals and protects our salvation once we are born again of the Spirit of God. All of these things are unmerited gifts from God, designed for our salvation. Grace is the unearned gift of God, one that is available to all His children of creation, regardless of who they are or what they have done. God's grace is a blessing that includes His mercy, His favor, His clemency, His reprieve, and His forgiveness. Grace was born out of God's great love and compassion. One afternoon, I was engaged in battle with my old enemy, fear, when the Holy Spirit broke into my thoughts with this revelation: "It is not fear that stops people from sinning; it is my love." The law fills our souls with the desire to rebel and triggers our fear of judgment. Grace, on the other hand, humbles our souls and fills us with the knowledge of God's great love. God's love is a powerful thing that can melt a heart of stone, destroy the desire to sin, and deliver us from all fear.

The Great Cost of Grace

One of my mottoes is that nothing in life comes without a cost. Every time we make a decision, we choose one thing or way over another. In so doing, we lose the object or way we rejected. As an example, if we choose not to have children, then we lose the experience of being a parent. If there comes a time when we are given something for nothing, we can be sure that someone else paid the price to make it available to us. The gift of salvation is no different. The gift of God's grace doesn't cost us anything; however, it is the most costly gift ever given. But God has paid the price for it. This is true on two levels. First, to make salvation available, Christ had to pay the price to atone for the sin of all humankind. The horrible price was the suffering and death of God's only Son.

The second cost comes with our God-given free will, which makes it necessary for each individual to choose to accept or reject God's gift of salvation. However, getting humankind to accept His great gift is an enormous challenge. It is the reason for everything God does in this world for His fallen children. It is the reason for God's long history of dealing with humankind, persevering with us to teach and woo us so we might choose to follow Him and accept His gift of salvation. It is the reason He gave humankind the Ten Commandments, sent the prophets of the Old Testament to declare His will, and sent His only Son to die an awful death to atone for sin. To this day, God is relentless in His loving pursuit of all His children of creation. He continues to anoint men and women to spread the gospel of salvation through Christ Jesus, all in an effort to woo us to believe Him and accept His gift.

Where Are Love and Grace?
(Relevant Scriptures: Genesis 19:1–29; Romans 8:22)

Some of God's actions directed at the people of the Old Testament may fill us with awe-inspired fear and take our breath away. He destroyed everyone but one family in a great flood. He went with the armies of His chosen people, giving them victory over those who stubbornly followed evil ways. He destroyed the cities of Sodom and Gomorrah because their citizens were sinful. In my quest to understand and trust God, I had to confront this question: Where is the love and grace in some of the actions God has taken against humankind? You can imagine my surprise when the revelation came to me that these and many other examples are all acts of grace and signs of God's relentless pursuit of and great love for His fallen children.

To understand this, we must realize that God's view of things is not limited to this natural, created world. He is the God of this world and of the spiritual-realm world. At the beginning of this book, I listed some things that God cannot do, with the exceptions that God cannot change who He is and cannot interfere with our freedom of choice. All other restrictions upon Him are self-imposed. They exist because God chose to find a way for us to reunite with Him. He could have left His spiritual-realm children separated from Him for all eternity, He could have decided to destroy this entire world any time He wanted, or He could have left this Earth behind and allowed us to destroy ourselves. He doesn't do these things because He made covenants with us and decided to give us the opportunity to accept His Way of salvation.

I do not know why it is so, but we humans often look at the punishment given to the guilty instead of focusing on the suffering of sin's victims. Perhaps it is because deep in our souls we know we are sinful and guilty of many sins ourselves. The ugliest truth about sin is that many times, the one who commits the sin is not the one who pays the price for it. At some points in history, evil overtook humankind so completely that God took those involved out of this world because the consequences of their actions were dreadful. God has destroyed whole populations as well as individuals. However, this does not mean that God threw all these individuals into the pits of hell in the spiritual realm. What it means is that God cleansed this natural-realm world in order to protect it and so it would continue until the purposes of this world were completed. God deals with all those individuals who were destroyed in the process on the other side, in the spiritual-realm world. This is another reason why I believe that the third area of the spiritual realm is critical for God's purposes.

God is love, and everything He does is done in love. It may be hard to see some of His actions as loving, but once you do, you know that His decisions are always for our good. Sometimes in my life, people's inhumane treatment of other people overwhelms me. I cry out to the Lord, asking Him to stop the world and let me get off. In those moments, I no longer want to be a part of this sin-filled world. So if I, with my puny love and care for others, have times when I want to leave this world behind, then what is the cost to God, who sees every vile, evil act and has witnessed the consequences of evil ever since the fall of Adam and Eve? It is by His grace that God perseveres with humankind until His plan of salvation is completely fulfilled. The entire world groans as we wait for the fulfillment of God's promises. Through the gift of His grace, He suffers along with us. He is going to get us through this by His great love and relentless pursuit of us. The day will come when He will bring an end to sin and suffering. He perseveres with us now at a great cost to Himself because it is His desire that all come to Him and receive salvation and freedom from the sinful nature that lives within human beings.

God's Plan of Salvation Has Always Been through Faith

(Relevant Scriptures: Galatians 3; Romans 9:30–33; Genesis 15:1–6, 16:1–15, 18:1–15, 22:1–19; Romans 4:13–25)

Long before God gave humankind the old covenant of the law and the new covenant of grace, He had a covenant with Abraham. To Abraham and his wife, Sarah, God first revealed that salvation would come through God's own direct supernatural intervention and not through the efforts of humankind. Instead, the atonement for sin would come through believing God and having faith in His method of redemption. Abraham was a man of faith who had obeyed God for many years. There was a great sadness in his life because Sarah was unable to conceive a child, so Abraham, in his old age, was without an heir or the hope of future descendants. One starry night, God promised Abraham that he would have a child by his own body and that his descendants would be as many as the stars in the sky, more than was possible to count. This was God's covenant with Abraham, and it was a startling promise from God, considering that Sarah was unable to conceive a child. Nevertheless, Abraham believed God, which was credited to him as righteousness.

As time passed and there was no child, Sarah decided that Abraham should have a child with her maidservant and that they could build a family in that way. The couple tried to fulfill God's promise of descendants through their own actions. When Abraham was eighty years old, Hagar, the maidservant, gave birth to his firstborn son, Ishmael. This did not work out well and brought much strife into the married couple's home. It was some years later that three visitors came to give Abraham the message that Sarah would soon give birth to a child even though she was long past her childbearing years. She did give birth to a son and named him Isaac. Isaac, the fulfillment of God's covenant with Abraham, was conceived through God's supernatural intervention, which defies the laws of nature.

Isaac was a much-loved child. When he was about twelve, God tested Abraham's faith by asking him to take Isaac up a mountain to make a blood sacrifice to atone for sin. God instructed Abraham not to take a sacrificial animal because He was going to provide the blood sacrifice. When the time came, God told Abraham that Isaac, his son, was to be the blood sacrifice that day. Abraham's precious child, who was the only way Abraham would have descendants and also the fulfillment of God's covenant, was to be killed. In horror, Abraham prepared to sacrifice his son. As he raised the knife over his boy, God spoke: "Do not kill him." There in the brush was a ram, the substitute for Isaac as a blood sacrifice for the forgiveness of sin.

This story tells us many things, but, for the purposes of this book, it shows us that the atonement for sin comes only through death and, even worse, the death of a son. It reveals that God would provide that sacrifice for sin, not through Abraham's son but through another supernaturally conceived child, God's very own Son. It was by Abraham's faith in God that Isaac was saved. Isaac lived to fulfill God's promise that Abraham would have many descendants. However, the true descendants of Abraham, more numerous than the stars in the sky, are not the children of Isaac, but all those who believe in God and in faith accept Jesus, God's sacrificial lamb for the atonement of sin. God made his covenant with Abraham long before he gave Moses the law and it is based on a promised child and God's supernatural intervention. It was a covenant based on faith in God and what He has done, not on what we do in obeying the law. It was because of Abraham's faith in God's provision that he became the father of all believers.

The Gospel of the Good News of Salvation through Jesus
(Relevant Scriptures: Romans 7:4–6; Galatians 2:15–21)

Righteousness is the goal of the law, so making us righteous would be the fulfillment of the law. It is through the sacrifice of Jesus that the old covenant of the law was fulfilled. When Jesus declared that He came to fulfill the law, He was telling us the incredibly good news that He came to make us righteous. He came to do for us what is impossible for us to do for ourselves. Thus, we are saved by His righteousness and not by any righteousness of our own gained by obeying the law. In other words, salvation is a result of what Jesus has done, not what we do. It is through God's grace that humankind has one ultimate commandment that must be obeyed to receive our salvation. It is God's highest commandment that we believe in and accept Jesus, His only begotten Son, for it is through Him that the demands of the law are satisfied and the entire law is fulfilled. This is the gospel of the good news of salvation through Jesus.

It's Just Too Good to Be True

The problem we have with this is that, sometimes, good news is just too good to be true. The good news of salvation in Jesus is like that; it is so straightforward and opposite to how we function in this world that it is hard to believe something so simple. We are so accustomed to the system of the world and so entrenched in the knowledge of good and evil that it can take us a very long time even after we have accepted Jesus to realize that our salvation is secure in Him. We have a tendency to want to add to the list of what is required to receive our salvation. This is where we miss the blessing of knowing that our eternal salvation is forever and that we are secure in Christ Jesus from the moment we accept Him.

You Cannot Mix the Covenants of Law and Grace
(Relevant Scripture: Matthew 9:17)

Jesus warned us about mixing the two covenants in a story about wineskins. Apparently, new wine could not be put into an old wineskin because it would burst. New wine had to have new wineskins because the old wineskins could not withstand the aging process of the new wine. Whenever this was attempted, the old wineskin was destroyed by the new wine and the wine spilled out. It is the same when we attempt to combine the old covenant of the law and the new covenant of grace. The Ten Commandments certainly have a place in a Christian's life, but they are never the agent of salvation. When we mix law and grace in regards to a believer's eternal salvation in Christ Jesus, we weaken the power of God's grace and stunt the believer's spiritual growth, at the same time distorting the true purpose of the Ten Commandments.

The proper use of the Ten Commandments in the Church is the same as it has always been. It is the mirror that reflects both God's righteousness and our sinfulness. The commandments provide parameters for our behavior, to which we can adhere and receive some protection from the consequences of sin until the time when sin is completely defeated. It is the means we can use to help us have happier lives. The Ten Commandments can be used to help those who have strayed away from right living and also as a guide to help lead unbelievers to accept Jesus. However, they can never be used as a way to eternal salvation in God or become mixed with the new covenant of grace.

One of the most beautiful revelations I received was about how Jesus completely fulfilled the Ten Commandments and then transformed them for all who have accepted Him as their Savior. Through the sacrifice of Christ Jesus and only for those who have accepted Him, the Ten Commandments also become the ten promises. They are His promise that He will complete in you what He started. He promises that the day will come, through the power of the Holy Spirit, when His children of salvation will be completely free of the sin that lives in them and become like Christ. In other words, believers will be able, through their actions and in their hearts, to fulfill those commandments. The time will come when we will be able to love the Lord our God with all our hearts. We will enter into Sabbath rest and will have no other gods but Him. In addition, we will not break any of the "thou shall not" commandments. We will not sin because the source of sin will be gone. We will be free of sin in our words, deeds, and hearts.

When I teach this, the response I most often hear is, "You mean a person can simply accept Jesus as their Savior, and then just go on to sin in any way they want, and still be saved?" If we look at this statement closely, we find that it is an exclamation of, "That's not fair! You mean that some people get to sin all they want, have a great time, and be saved while I try to live in obedience to

God?" Indignation almost always accompanies this train of thought, suggesting that sin is a fun thing that has no consequences.

When we think like this, we fail to realize that we all keep sinning after we are saved. When the Holy Spirit severs the sinful nature's lifeline from a person's heart, the sinful nature begins to shrivel and die. However, it does not completely die until the body dies. This means that it continues to influence us, leading us to sin—sometimes through our conscious decisions and sometimes unbeknownst to us. What we must remember is that sin always comes with consequences. Those who accept Jesus as their Savior and then proceed to sin deliberately are making for themselves a life filled with trouble and turmoil. These people are subject not only to the consequences of sin but also to the discipline of the Lord until they repent of their ways and obey God.

There are those believers who do continue to commit grievous sin after they have accepted Jesus; however, they will not continue to sin forever. God accepts all of us when we come to Him for salvation, regardless of our condition and circumstances. We don't all start in the same place, and we are not instantly set free of the sins that so easily overtake us. Some of us start our new life in Christ as children of believers who have learned the Ten Commandments and known about Jesus all their lives. Others have been damaged or abused or come from other faiths. Some others are simply willful and unyielding.

As I was driving down a beautiful tree-lined street in late fall, all of the trees were bare of their leaves and looked totally dead. If I were a foreigner from another world, I would think that those trees were without life. It is the same when we attempt to declare others lost and separated from God by looking only at their behavior. On the one hand, there are those who live exemplary lives and whose good behavior hides the fact that they have not accepted Jesus as their Savior. Then there are those whose bad behavior is readily visible, but at some moment in time, they sincerely asked Jesus to be their Savior. Only God may judge them. However, we can be sure of this one thing: if they have not accepted their salvation in Jesus, then the Holy Spirit is pursuing them from the outside; and if they have accepted their salvation, then the Holy Spirit is at work in their hearts correcting the problem, whatever it may be. The truth is that very often, the consequences of our sin combined with the Holy Spirit's love and discipline finally stops us from following the sinful nature. While we may perceive someone as being on the road to a fall, that person's bad behavior may finally turn him or her from sin. Shockingly, the unbeliever who behaves better is in the most danger of rejecting Christ. This type of individual may be trapped in an "I am a good person" mind-set, which has hidden dangers for an unbeliever. Cult leaders are masters of misleading people to adopt this kind of mind-set, one that can lead others away from the need to accept Christ Jesus.

While it is certainly true that our behavior does affect our walk with the Lord, the quality of our life on Earth, our rewards in heaven, and the position we will hold as we begin our spiritual life there, it is also true for those who have accepted Christ as their Savior that their behavior cannot affect the righteousness of Christ Jesus. Remember, it is by His righteousness that we are saved. No matter how well you keep the laws before you are a Christian and no matter how well you keep them after you become a Christian, it is still the righteousness of Christ that satisfies the demands of the law, provides the covering for sin, and opens the way for the Holy Spirit to dwell within you.

The good news is that once you are born again of the Spirit of God, it cannot be undone because you are now His child of salvation. Your eternal salvation depends on what Jesus did for you. You have made an irrevocable decision and put Christ Jesus in charge of your salvation. In addition, we must also understand that our salvation in Jesus is protected and guarded by the power of the Holy Spirit within us. If we are to live in the security of the salvation Jesus died to provide for us, then we must build our faith on a firm foundation, understanding the certainty of salvation we have in Him.

CHAPTER 14

LIVING UNDER THE NEW COVENANT OF GRACE

(Relevant Scripture: Isaiah 64:6)

While I was having lunch with a dear friend, she asked me to explain if salvation is a gift or a work. This question had been the topic of discussion in the adult Sunday school class at her church. The subject is often a point of some confusion, and discussions about it can result in a merry-go-round of conflicting Scripture references. Some Scriptures inform us that salvation is a gift from God, not something earned by works. One Scripture even likens our good works to filthy rags. Add to this the Scriptures that deal with obeying God, living right, and asking Christians to do good works, and you have a mix of seemingly opposite statements. All this can lead us to adopt a works-based doctrine and keep us from living in the security of our salvation in Christ

Jesus. A believer may be misguided about faith versus works unless he or she clearly understands that salvation operates in two stages. In stage one, we are justified by Christ and receive our eternal life in Him. In stage two, we are sanctified by the Holy Spirit and begin our new life in Christ living in God's kingdom. Once we know how these two stages of salvation function, the Scriptures fall into their rightful places and we can live more fully and powerfully under the new covenant of grace.

Stage One: The Gift of Salvation
(Relevant Scriptures: Romans 10:8–13; Ephesians 2:8–9; John 6:37–40; John 19:30; Acts 13:38–39; Ephesians 1:13–14; Colossians 2:9–11)

Stage one of salvation is accomplished when we hear the gospel of Christ Jesus, believe it to be true, and accept Jesus as our Savior. Having believed in our hearts, we are born again of the Spirit of God and are now a new creation. We have accepted the atonement for sin; in so doing, we are now justified by Christ and are covered in His righteousness. The process of making the decision to believe the gospel is over. Jesus clearly states, "The work of God is this: to believe in the one he has sent" (John 6:29). Once we believe in Jesus, we accept the One whom God the Father sent to save us. In other words, our new life in Christ begins and we live under the new covenant of grace.

This first stage of salvation is all about accepting God's gift of salvation. It is God's perfect and unspeakable gift, made available by the life, sacrifice, death, and resurrection of Jesus Christ. It cannot be earned, and nothing can be added to it. All we can do is either accept it or reject it.

Once we accept the gift of salvation, stage one of salvation is completed. Just before Jesus died on the cross, He pronounced, "It is finished." With this statement, Jesus proclaimed that He had done all that was necessary to save humanity. When we accept His sacrifice for our salvation, "It is finished." We take into ourselves everything that is necessary for our personal salvation. In other words, all the essential things needed for our salvation have already been provided. The process of coming to believe that Jesus is God and the Savior of the world is realized and we accept him as our Savior. The onetime overall repentance, or turning away from sin, is complete and we are thereby forgiven of our sins, past, present, and future. Most important, we show that we have obeyed God's ultimate commandment to believe in and accept His Son; in so doing, we become an obedient child of salvation in whom the law has been fulfilled. The Holy Spirit has entered the heart area of our souls and cut the life supply of the sinful nature, which begins the process of freeing us from the power of the sinful nature. In addition, the Holy Spirit has diffused through our own spirit, making us born again of the Spirit of God. At this point, our salvation is sealed by the Holy Spirit and remains under His protection. This safeguards our eternal life in Christ and secures forever our eternal destination in God's heavenly kingdom. I have often used the following lighthearted statement to get this point across: "Once you have accepted Jesus as your Savior, you are going to go to heaven—and there is nothing you can do about it." As Christians, we must always remember that it is Jesus who is going to present us as holy and acceptable before the throne of God. He is our salvation.

Jesus Is the Cornerstone
(Relevant Scriptures: Ephesians 2:19–22; Hosea 6:6 Living Bible)

Jesus is the cornerstone of our salvation. He is the stone upon which we must build our lives and our faith. If we do not completely understand that our salvation is complete and secured in Him, then we will build our faith on a flawed and shaky foundation. This results in a confusing mix of grace- and works-oriented salvation, which distorts our faith and interferes with the Holy Spirit's work within us. It also has the sad effect of robbing us of the humble confidence God wants us to have as He lovingly cares for us.

For humans, it is easy to jump to the conclusion that the biggest challenge God faces with His children of salvation is getting them to stop sinning. While that is certainly part of His ministry, He has a much harder time getting us to trust Him and know His all-encompassing love. The most tragic consequence of this is that knowing God and His love for us is the most awesome power for change hidden in grace. God's grace and love will change a person's heart, turning it from sin faster than any commandment or rule ever could. Knowing God's love brings us into Sabbath rest and causes us to submit our will to Him. Here, I will repeat one of my most favorite Scriptures from *The Living Bible*. God cries out, "I don't want your sacrifices—I want your love; I don't want your offerings—I want you to know me" (Hosea 6:6 Living Bible). God knows that we can never completely love and worship Him if we do not know Him and His great love for us. As God's children of salvation, our main focus should be seeking to know God and His love for us.

I received a vision one afternoon when the Holy Spirit was trying to teach me to trust Him to complete what He had begun in me. I saw myself in an elevator that was taking me to where I wanted go, yet in that elevator, I was trying to climb up the walls in an effort to get to where the elevator was already taking me. This is a graphic picture of how foolish it is for a Christian to believe that his or her salvation in Christ is achieved through works. The sad thing was, as far as my eternal destination was concerned, I was already where I wanted to be. I was safe and secure in Jesus and destined to spend all eternity in His heavenly kingdom. Once we accept Jesus as our Savior, that is where we all are. We begin our life in the kingdom of God totally and completely forgiven—and our citizenship in His kingdom is secured and sealed for all eternity.

The Gift of Freedom
(Relevant Scripture: Romans 6:1–14)

In stage one of salvation; we are released to begin our new life in God's kingdom. A child of salvation possesses many freedoms. Among these are freedom from the guilt of sin (because we have been forgiven), the penalty of sin (because Jesus paid the price for us), and the power of sin (because the Holy Spirit has circumcised our hearts, severing the lifeline to the sinful nature). We are also free from the curse of the law and live under the new covenant of grace. The moment we accept Jesus, we are free from the permanent, eternal separation from God and the permanent, eternal consequences of sin. It is important to understand that salvation is not a license to abandon ourselves to sin without any consequences; instead, it is a ticket out of sin. There are always consequences of sin; however, for the Christian, those consequences do not include losing salvation in Christ Jesus. Stage one of salvation is all about accepting the gift of salvation and securing our eternal destination in God's heavenly kingdom. We begin the second stage of salvation as a free, forgiven, born-again child of salvation and a citizen of God's heavenly kingdom who is destined to spend all eternity in our heavenly Father's presence.

Stage Two: Unwrapping the Gift of Salvation
(Relevant Scriptures: Proverbs 18:16; John 6:29, 13:1–10; Philippians 2:12–13; Romans 11:5–6; 1 John 3:1–2)

The baby Jesus was wrapped in swaddling clothes and laid in a manager, and God's gift of salvation was presented to the world. The Scriptures do not say that Mary dressed her newborn baby; instead, He was wrapped like any wonderful gift would be. Once we have accepted this great gift, the only thing left for us to do is unwrap the gift we already possess and discover what wonders are contained inside. If you can call that work, then it is the work of salvation; however, it is never the work to achieve or earn salvation. You may also regard your salvation as a treasure chest. You own the chest and no one can take it away from you, so you open the chest and find the treasures hidden there. The second stage of salvation is about living out our salvation by learning to apply all the benefits we received when we accepted the gift of salvation.

While stage one is about what Jesus has done for us, stage two is centered on the work of the Holy Spirit within us and the ongoing process of sanctification. What Jesus has already done for us is put into action inside of us by way of the Holy Spirit. Stage two is all about learning how to live in God's kingdom while we live in this world. It is in this stage that we become partners with the Holy Spirit in applying all the tools and benefits of the gift of salvation. Unfortunately, we may become confused and begin to think that we must work to be saved or to keep our salvation when we are in stage two. This is a tragic distortion of the truth.

The Scriptures do not tell us to work for our salvation; instead, they instruct us to "continue to work out your salvation" (Philippians 2:12). Sanctification is each individual's personal living out or working out of the salvation he or she already possesses. No one ever works to own what is already theirs. Instead, they work to utilize and build upon what they already possess. Dr. Warren W. Wiersbe explains it this way in *The Bible Exposition Commentary:* "The verb 'work out' carries the meaning of 'work to full completion,' such as working out a problem in mathematics. In Paul's day it was also used for 'working a mine,' that is, getting out of the mine all the valuable ore possible, or 'working a field' so as to get the greatest harvest possible."

In stage two, we begin the process of actually becoming good, instead of merely trying to be good. We learn to follow the Holy Spirit as He leads us into the wonders of our salvation. It is through our relationship with and the ministry of the Holy Spirit within us that the internal change of the heart begins to take place. In stage two of salvation, everything, the good, the bad, and the ugly, is in the process of being transformed by God, who uses everything for our benefit. In other words, this is our journey out of sin and into freedom from sin. It is also a time of healing and release from the damage that sin has inflicted upon us. This includes the individual sins we have committed, the suffering we've endured because of the sins of others, and the damage we've experienced just from living in this sin-filled world.

We all begin our new lives in God's kingdom in different places and circumstances. We bring with us doubts, fears, confusion, indifference, and sinful behavior. Most of us enter the second stage of salvation with a limited understanding of exactly what is contained in the gift of salvation. Often, we simply accept the gift and place it on some shelf in our soul, leaving it unopened for years. It sits there waiting for the day when we leave this world and go to heaven. We have our salvation in Christ, but we are living in this world without receiving the full benefits of the gift because we have not opened it. The problem with this is in stage two, we are to become partners with God. If we do not do our part, then we stunt our spiritual growth and miss the many blessings contained in the gift of salvation. This does not mean that we lose our salvation, but it does mean that we are not living and enjoying the full blessings of our salvation now as we live on Earth.

In stage two, we begin to develop an ongoing relationship with the Holy Spirit. One wonderful Scripture states, "A gift opens the way for the giver and ushers him into the presence of the great" (Proverbs 18:16). The gift of salvation does just that. God's gift of salvation, through the sacrifice of Christ Jesus, opens the Way for the Holy Spirit to dwell within us and ushers Him into our presence. This is when we begin the process that Scripture calls "walking by the Spirit." (Galatians 5:25) The word *walking* implies movement and progression. We are moving toward becoming like Christ and maturing spiritually in our relationship with the Holy Spirit. It is in this stage that we can do things that help us grow in our knowledge of and relationship with God. If we simply accept the gift of salvation and never put forth the effort to unwrap the gift, then we slow the rate of our spiritual growth and miss many of the awesome benefits that are part and parcel of salvation.

When we were born into this world, we grew in the knowledge of this world and learned its ways. When we are born again of God's Spirit, we enter the spiritual realm and begin to grow spiritually in the knowledge and principles of that world. We have the awesome opportunity to begin the process of coming to know God (not simply knowing about Him). In other words, we are to become seekers of a relationship with the Holy Spirit. During this process, we can learn to give ourselves to God and submit to the Holy Spirit within us. It is never too late to get started. It is the adventure of a lifetime. I have never explained to anyone how I overcame the mental turmoil and spiritual battle I experienced, but I can tell you this: I simply walked out of it by "walking in the Spirit" and using the tools and gifts of the Holy Spirit that were made available to me in the gift of salvation. It wasn't easy. I had a great deal of help from the Holy Spirit and those wonderful people He sent to assist me. However, it was the walk of a lifetime—one of the most wonderful blessings of my life.

During the Last Supper before Jesus was crucified, He washed his disciples' feet. When Jesus came to Peter, the following exchange took place. "'No,' said Peter, 'you shall never wash my feet.' Jesus answered, 'Unless I wash you, you have no part with me.' 'Then, Lord,' Simon Peter replied, 'not just my feet but my hands and my head as well!' Jesus answered, 'A person who has had a bath needs only to wash his feet; his whole body is clean'" (John 13:8–10). This exchange explains the two kinds of cleansings we receive through Jesus. The first washing away of our sin is done once and is for all our sins, past, present, and future. This happens when we accept Jesus as our Savior. In so doing, we receive the bath through the atonement for sin. The second washing is the ongoing cleansing needed to keep us clean of the effects of sin as we walk through this world. I love this picture. Feet are made for walking. The second stage of salvation consists of "walking in the Spirit," but it also entails walking through this sinful world, where the sinful nature still influences us even though it is in the process of dying. Living out our salvation as we live in this world is a messy thing. Jesus, in His endearing way, is teaching us that His cleansing of sin is ongoing as we walk with Him through this world.

Connie Becker

The Tools of Salvation
(Relevant Scriptures: Galatians 5:16–25; Romans 8:26; 1 Corinthians 2:10–12; John 8:12)

The second stage of salvation is a glorious time, but it is not always an easy time. As Christians, we live in a position of conflict. We have the Holy Spirit dwelling within us, but we also have the sinful nature still harbored in our souls. Many times, it does feel like an angel is on one shoulder and the Devil is on the other, the two of them competing to influence our decisions and behavior. For a forgiven child of salvation in this sinful world, life can be full of conflict and uncertainty. This is another reason why it is so important to understand that our eternal salvation in Christ is secure. It gives us the confidence to move forward into the things of God and, at the same time, trust Him with all our faults and mishaps as we seek to follow Him. The conflict, along with any sins we may commit and other things this world dishes out, can easily overwhelm our souls and interfere with our relationship with the Holy Spirit. We do not begin our life in Christ as mature Christians; we begin as spiritual babies recently born into the spiritual-realm world. We have to grow in our knowledge of God as we live in His grace. In order to help with this conflict and the journey of our spiritual growth, the Lord has given us sacred sacraments and different methods that when properly applied can be used as the means to help our souls remain calm and confident before Him. I have come to think of these sacraments and methods as powerful tools of the Christian faith. Using these tools in faith helps us to grow spiritually and in our relationship with Him.

The sacraments and methods include communion, confession, worship, prayer, Bible study and fellowship with other believers. These practices are common in the church and are so familiar to us that it is easy to forget that they are made powerful through the ministry of the Holy Spirit within us. In other words, they are touched by the Holy Spirit and are used for our spiritual and mental well-being. These tools are not given to Christians to accomplish salvation or to allow us to keep our salvation. Instead, they strengthen us in our salvation and deepen our walk with the Lord. They are there to enable us to live the abundant life of peace and joy that God longs for us to enjoy.

Communion

(Relevant Scriptures: 1 Corinthians 11:25–26; Matthew 26:26–28)

At the Last Supper, Jesus held up the bread, saying, "Take and eat; this is my body." Then he took the cup, gave thanks and offered it to them, saying, "Drink from it, all of you. This is my blood of the covenant, which is poured out for many for the forgiveness of sins" (Matthew 26:26–28). What a powerful picture this is for all believers. It relates all the way back to Adam and Eve, when, in an act of disobedience, they ate the forbidden fruit, ingesting into themselves the sinful nature. When we accept the gift of salvation given to us through the sacrifice of Jesus, we ingest or take into ourselves the nature of God and are reunited with His Spirit. Communion is something we do in remembrance of Jesus and what He has done for us. Using the bread and the wine, Jesus gave us the sacrament of Communion to remind us that through the death of His body and sacrifice of His blood, our sins are forever covered and His life lives in us.

I spent over thirty years attending Lutheran churches. They handle the sacrament of Communion in the most personal way. Row by row, the people come to the altar, kneel down, and receive the bread and the wine. For a few years, I assisted in the giving of Communion. As the pastor gave the bread, he would say over each individual, "The body of Christ given for you." I would follow with the wine speaking over each person: "The blood of Jesus shed for you." It was a personal moment between each person and the Holy Spirit. I can tell you that very often, as I said those words over people, I could feel the power of the Holy Spirit going out to them.

Confession
(Relevant Scriptures: Romans 7:14–19; Philippians 2:11; 1John 1:8–9; Hebrews 13:15; Luke 18:9–14; Philippians 3:13–14; Romans 10:8-10)

Another powerful tool is the practice of confession. It is hard to overstate the importance of confession in a Christian's life. It is a valuable tool that functions on two levels. (1) We make a positive confession of our belief and confidence in Jesus and what He has done for us. (2) We confess of sin and those things that are affecting our faith in a negative way. Because confession involves the act of speaking, hearing is part of the process of confessing. It was through hearing the gospel of Christ that we came to believe; in the same way, it is through hearing our confessions that we may communicate with our souls and spirits as well as with God. On the one hand, we are expressing to God our faith in Him as we hear our own confession, it solidifies our faith. On the other hand, when we hear our confession of sin, we enable our souls and spirits to release the guilt and disappointment we have about the things we have done or are struggling with or that are weighing us down. The main purpose of confession is to keep the channel between ourselves and God open so that we may enjoy a closer walk with Him. God does not want us carrying around a load of sin and guilt. He wants us free to follow Him in joy and humble confidence of His loving care.

The apostle Paul writes about how frustrating and difficult it can be to deal with our sinfulness after we've accepted Christ. He laments, "For I have the desire to do what is good, but I cannot carry it out. For what I do is not the good I want to do; no, the evil I do not want to do—this I keep doing" (Romans 7:19). As we grow in our salvation, our desires start to change and we begin to seek to live free of sin. When we fall or find our behavior un-Christ-like, the guilt and frustration threaten to overcome us. Guilt, regret, and condemnation can cause us to have shame before God, which interferes with our relationship with Him. It can even open a door for Satan to accuse us, causing us to experience upset and confusion. Confession of sin brings it openly to God and makes a way for our souls to be healed and restored. When we follow confession of sin with confession of our confidence in God's forgiveness, it calms our conscious minds, hearts, and spirits.

In stage one when we accept Jesus as our savior. We confess that we are sinners, in need of a savior. In so doing, we make a one-time overall confession of our sin. We then confess our acceptance of Jesus as our savior and our faith in Him. In stage two of salvation confession of sin is very much like foot washing. It is the method of cleansing of the soul and spirit of the debris that accumulates as we live in this world. God wants us free of this debris so we can more fully communicate with Him and live more abundantly in the blessings of our salvation. God does not use confession so He can forgive us, for He has already done that. Instead, he uses confession to release us from the internal consequences of sin. He gives us the tool of confession to help us accept His forgiveness so that we can continue to move forward in Him. As Paul writes, "Forgetting what is behind and straining toward what is ahead. I press on toward the goal to win the prize for which God has called me heavenward in Christ Jesus" (Philippians 3:13–14). Once we have accepted Jesus and confessed our faith in him the goal of confession changes for the believer. In the above scripture Paul is not speaking of salvation as the goal because he already had his salvation. Instead, the goal is progressing in the knowledge of the spiritual realm and growing closer in our relationship with God, becoming more and more Christ-like.

Fellowship of Believers
(Relevant Scriptures: James 5:16; 1 John 1:7; Hebrews 10:25; Romans 12:9–12; Colossians 3:15–16; Acts 1:14)

I knew a sweet Christian woman who, in a time of trouble, said to me, "Sometimes you need someone in a body." What she meant is that sometimes God can seem far away and we need someone we can see and touch to help us. The Lord knows that we humans need that kind of interaction. In the fifth chapter of the book of James, we are encouraged to confess our sins to one another so we can be healed. There is something very powerful about speaking out our problems to another person. It would be impossible for me to remember how many times I have called a friend when I have been unhappy with myself or have had some problem that I needed to talk out. Telling a good friend seems to help me get past it and let go of it.

As believers, we have a common bond in Christ. We are part of the family of God. This opens the door for us to be strengthened and supported in our daily walk through this world and with the Lord. It increases our ability to grow spiritually because we are grouped together, which opens the way for us to utilize all of the tools and methods given to us as believers. We do not all grow at the same rate, and we all have been given different experiences, understanding, and gifts. When we draw on other believers' knowledge and gifts, it strengthens our faith and we grow in our relationship with the Lord. We can pray together, worship together, and study the Scriptures, with the more mature Christians teaching the newer believers. This helps us to pool our resources and talents for the good of our Christian brothers and sisters as well as the world community. The Christian life was not meant to be lived in seclusion, apart from other believers. The Church was formed so that believers could come together, seeking the presence of the Lord, and tending to each other's needs.

It was not long after I slipped into mental and spiritual turmoil that my family had to move to another city. My stress level was already out of sight. It took every ounce of strength I had to make the move, but I am so thankful that we did. Never in my life was I more certain that I was exactly where I was supposed to be. Waiting for me in my new hometown were five wonderful women who came together to form a prayer group. These loving and Spirit-filled women of faith were one of the Lord's great gifts to me. It is through these women that I came to know a new level of Christianity. They were aware of the Holy Spirit within them, and they submitted to Him and

His gifts. They opened up a whole new world of faith to me and helped me to overcome my mental illness and win my spiritual battle. When we open ourselves to the Holy Spirit and fellowship together in word and in prayer, we can expect miracles. I know this because it is a miracle that I survived; however, I not only survived, but I also thrived. It was not long before I joined the ranks of those Spirit-filled women.

Prayer

(Relevant Scriptures: Deuteronomy 4:7; Matthew 6:5–13, 7:7–11, 18:18–20; 1 Thessalonians 5:16–17; James 5:13–16; Romans 8:26–27; Ephesians 6:18; Philippians 4:6–7; John 14:12–14; Luke 11:9)

Whenever I seek to define prayer, I am left with the uneasy feeling that what I have provided amounts only to a description of prayer, not a definition of it. This is because prayer operates on so many different levels and reaches into the spiritual realm. I am aware that prayer is deeper than my ability to explain it. It is relatively simple to list the different kinds of prayer: communication and petition; praise and worship; and confession of sin and confession of faith. It is used in spiritual warfare and to intercede for other people. Because there is such a wide range of prayer, it can be defined as anything from worship to simply wishing. This is because prayer is a tool that is available in the natural-realm world and reaches into the spiritual-realm world. This has led me to define prayer in this way: Prayer is the vehicle of spiritual communion with God. It is the line of communication between God and humankind that allows the interaction between the natural, created-realm world in which we live and the spiritual-realm world where God resides. The more we grow spiritually, and the deeper our relationship with the Holy Spirit becomes, Christians come to live in an atmosphere of prayer.

The most simplistic way of defining prayer is as "reaching out to God." Prayer is among one of the most instinctive things human beings do. We are born with an innate need to find God and communicate with Him. Prayer is so intricately woven into the fabric of the Christian faith that we sometimes forget that it, in some form, is part of every person's life. The remarkable thing is that God hears all prayer. He is omnipresent, meaning that He is everywhere at the same time—and He is waiting for His created children to reach out to Him. If this was not so, then how would anyone who has not yet accepted Christ ever make a connection with Him?

However, not all prayer is the same. Just as there are different types of prayer, there are also two different levels of prayer: non-Christian and Christians. The non-Christian's prayers operate on a completely different level than those offered up by people who have accepted Jesus as their Savior. This is because God surrounds unbelievers and hears their prayers from outside their bodies and souls.

The non-Christian does not have the intimate connection that the Christian enjoys, nor is there the same wisdom and power accompanying non-Christians' prayers. The prayers of the unbeliever are fundamentally a reaching out to God on the most elementary level.

The magnificent difference in the prayers of a Christian is that God hears them from within us. The Holy Spirit resides within the spirit, heart, and mind of the Christian. Thus, the Holy Spirit actually becomes the conduit of our prayers. As Christians, we pray to God the Father in the name of Jesus, His Son. The Holy Spirit is the channel through which our prayers flow directly to the throne room of God. This is a two-way communication that opens the way for the Holy Spirit to communicate God's will to us in reply. This not only gives us knowledge of how to pray, but also increases our faith and intimacy with God. The Holy Spirit opens the way for our prayers and relationship with God to be more powerful in terms of having an impact on our lives and on this natural-realm world.

Years ago, I read a statement about prayer that suggested that prayer should be approached in the same way a scientist preforms experiments. This changed how I approached prayer. I began learning how to pray and experimenting with different types of prayer. Martin Luther put it this way: "As a shoemaker makes a shoe and a tailor makes a coat, so should a Christian pray." Prayer is the business and the science of a Christian. Prayer is a practical thing. We are to continually learn how to pray more effectively. We are not to have one kind of prayer for all circumstances, nor are we to be content in not receiving answers to our prayers. We are to keep seeking to learn and to keep asking the Holy Spirit how to pray and how to submit to Him in prayer. In other words, we are to keep experimenting with prayer until it works. A few years ago, a billboard caught my attention. It showed a picture of Thomas Edison and a light bulb along with the caption, "After ten thousand tries, there was light." As Christians, we need to follow the example of this scientist.

Scripture clearly instructs believers to pray. We are told, "Ask and it shall be given you; seek and you will find; knock and the door will be open to you" (Luke 11:9). Two things are immediately apparent when I read these Scriptures. The first is the active relationship that we establish with God as we pray. The very process of asking and seeking makes possible God's response. Second, there is an intensity of action implied in these words.

When I was seeking a way out of my mental and spiritual difficulties, prayer became my main focus. I approached prayer as if my life depended on it. I asked and kept on asking. I continued to seek God in addition to information about my problems. I then prayed accordingly. I became open and honest with God. If I had a question, I asked it, and if I needed direction, I asked for it. If I was angry, I expressed it; if I was heartbroken, I told him about it. And if all I could do was cry, then I cried. I kept knocking on God's door with what I later described as "bloody knuckles knocking." Just as the Scriptures promised, I started to receive what I asked for; I found the answers I was seeking, and the door opened for me to have a deeper and more intimate relationship with the Holy Spirit. Does God want us always to pray with such intensity? No, but He does want us to actively come to Him, establish a relationship with Him through the Holy Spirit, and learn His will and His ways as we pray.

My Wednesday Prayer Group

For me, Wednesdays became an island in the middle of the week. This was when my five friends and I would meet for a time of sharing and prayer. Sometimes I didn't want to go on vacation because I would miss our meeting on Wednesday. We never knew exactly what to expect on Wednesdays. What my friends and I did know, however, was that our awareness of the presence of the Holy Spirit would increase and the gifts of the Holy Spirit would be manifested. Our prayers were more specific as we were given wisdom and knowledge of how to pray. As we praised and worshiped the Lord together, it was as if we could truly enter into His courts. At times, I could feel the power of my prayers leaving my body. At other times, I was aware of the healing taking place in my soul. I was not alone; all of us received answers to our prayers for ourselves and others. We all grew in our relationship with the Holy Spirit and our ability to submit to His leading.

When my youngest daughter was five, she started having repeated kidney infections caused by a condition called reflux. If this condition is serious enough, then surgery is performed to replace the valves in the kidneys. The doctors decided to watch the situation. For two years, my daughter did not have an infection. Then, at age seven, she had a bad infection. Again, tests were scheduled to determine a course of action. A foreboding feeling came over me; I knew that surgery might be the next step. I waited until everyone was asleep before I tiptoed into my daughter's room and gently laid my hands on her tummy. I asked the Lord to re-create her as He originally designed her to be. No bells or whistles went off. I had no special sense of God's presence, no sign at all that anything had happened when I prayed. I returned to my room and randomly opened my Bible to a story about the woman who had asked Jesus to heal her daughter. My eyes landed on the words, "And her daughter was healed from that very hour." (Matthew 15:28) As I read those words, a "knowing" came over me. I absolutely knew that my daughter had been healed. We kept our scheduled appointment, where she went through a complete urinary workup at the hospital. These tests confirmed that she was, indeed, completely healed. Not only was the reflux gone, but also all of the scar tissue that had shown up in previous X-rays was gone. She is now forty years old and, to this day, has not had a problem in this area.

Sometimes, following the Holy Spirit takes courage. The things of the spiritual realm seem strange to us and are often more than a little scary. I was bound by fear and could not seem to free myself; this led me finally to accept that there are certain prayers for that kind of thing. They are called deliverance prayers. It took courage, but I gathered the prayer group together one afternoon and we cast out the spirit of fear from my soul. We simply came against the fear in the name of Jesus and commanded it to leave. I literally felt it go. We asked the Holy Spirit to fill my soul and protect me from the return of my bondage in fear. I was freed. It was at that moment that I began to experience relief from my mental turmoil at a faster rate. The fear that had been holding me back now had a diminished effect on me. I was able to move forward with my healing. Fear still attacks me, but it has never again bound me. Now I know what to do when it does attack me.

Before I joined the prayer group, the Holy Spirit revealed to me that those vicious thought-attacks were not coming from me; they were coming from the Enemy of my soul. One of the first messages I received from the Holy Spirit was that I should answer those attacks with the words, "That is contrary to the Word of God." I will admit that, at the time, those words didn't feel like much help. It felt as if Satan was using guided missiles against me and I had a small squirt gun for my defense. The first thing I had to adjust to was the fact that Satan was attacking me, which in itself is scary. However, once I did this, I started to come against him in the name of Jesus and used the words that the Holy Spirit had revealed to me. It may have felt as if

I had a small weapon, but that little squirt gun was filled with the power of the Holy Spirit. When, in faith, I learned to use it, that weapon defeated the power of Satan's lies.

I learned many powerful ways to pray during my walk out of my soul sickness. I learned that the Holy Spirit can permeate deep into the soul and minister to the deep mind (the heart), the conscious mind, and even the memories. Through the power of prayer and our submission to His ways, He can heal our memories. He can go back to the moment when something traumatic happened and change our mental reaction to it. When He does this, it sets off a chain reaction that begins to heal us of the trauma that occurred in the soul. He does not take away the memory, but He changes the reaction, which allows the soul to begin to heal the injury. God cannot change what has touched us in this sin-filled world, but He can certainly transform it and release us from the consequences in our souls. This miraculous work of the Holy Spirit helped to change my sadness to joy.

A Closer Walk with the Holy Spirit
(Relevant Scriptures: Romans 8:14–16, 26–27; Revelation 3:20–22; Acts 2:4, 8:14–17, 9:17–18, 10:44–48; Matthew 3:11)

The tools of Communion, Bible study, confession, prayer, and fellowship with believers are all effective and powerful because they are anointed by the Holy Spirit. For instance, it is not enough to learn how to say the right words when we pray; instead, we must learn how to open up and submit to the leading of the Holy Spirit within us. God hears all our prayers and responds, but if we want to grow in prayer and our awareness of the Holy Spirit, then we must allow the Holy Spirit to lead us and empower us to pray.

Stage one of salvation is all about accepting Jesus. Stage two is all about submitting to the Holy Spirit and allowing Him to permeate into the deepest recesses of our being. At the same time, we are to allow Him access to the more conscious areas of our mind. This process is the same as that in stage one of salvation, only in reverse. In stage one, the Holy Spirit passes through the conscious areas of the soul and enters the heart area (deep mind) and the spirit. In stage two, the Holy Spirit seeks to permeate into all of the soul's recesses and reenter the conscious areas of the mind. This process, however, can be restricted if we do not give our permission and submit. Stage one of salvation took place because you asked Jesus to be your Savior. Stage two of salvation is enhanced and accelerated by asking the Holy Spirit to release Himself into the hidden closets of your heart and come into the conscious areas of your mind. This is what spiritual growth is all about. When we are instructed to, "Ask and it will be given to you, seek and you will find, knock and the door will be open to you," the directives apply as much to growing closer to the Holy Spirit as they do to accepting Jesus and receiving answers to our prayers.

This process is called the infilling of the Holy Spirit or the baptism of the Holy Spirit. All Christians have the Holy Spirit dwelling within them, and no one is given more of the Holy Spirit than another. However, if we want a more intimate relationship with Him, we must seek it through the process of asking, knocking, and using all the tools of salvation God has given us. This should be our main focus in the second stage of salvation. The closeness of our walk with the Lord depends on it and is the way in which God empowers each individual believer and the Church on Earth to do His will.

More Gifts
(Relevant Scriptures 1Corinthians 12: 7-11)

The tools of salvation listed above are not the only gifts available to Christians in the second stage of salvation. Also available are the nine manifested gifts of the Holy Spirit. They are the gift of His wisdom, knowledge, faith, healing, miracles, prophecy, discernment of spirits, speaking in tongues, and interpretation of tongues. The major difference between the gifts of the Holy Spirit and the tools of salvation is that they operate on different levels. The tools of salvation are for our use, enhanced and anointed by the Holy Spirit. The nine gifts of the Holy Spirit belong to Him and are direct manifestations of Him within us.

These gifts are activated only when we submit to the Holy Spirit and allow Him to flow through us. All too often, these gifts are not activated in believers as powerfully as they should be because they are more mysterious and people do not understand them. Because they are for the empowerment of the Church on Earth and for the individual believers who make up the body of Christ, it makes me sad that many believers don't actively pursue the manifestation gifts of the Holy Spirit. This causes believers to miss the opportunity to live a more dynamic life in partnership with the Holy Spirit.

Seeking to grow spiritually and submit to the flow of the Holy Spirit is important because it enhances all areas of our walk with the Lord. When we look at the gift of salvation as a pair of shoes made for walking in the Spirit, we get a clear picture of how important it is to open the entire gift of salvation. When we accept Jesus as our Savior, we receive the full pair of shoes. However, if we never open the second part of the gift of salvation, it is as if we put one shoe on a foot and carry the other in a box as we attempt to walk with the Holy Spirit. When we do this, we certainly have the entire gift of salvation, but we are not implementing it as we should. In doing this, we cripple ourselves and the Church and miss many of the wonderful blessings Jesus died to give us. I cannot overstate the importance that the manifestation of the Holy Spirit's gifts had to my recovery from the mental turmoil and spiritual battle I endured.

Connie Becker

Summary
(Relevant Scriptures: Ephesians 6:10–18; Romans 12:1–8; 1Corinthians 12:7-11))

God did not send us, his children of salvation, out into this world without providing us with all kinds of gifts and tools to use for our spiritual growth, protection, and healing, and for bringing others to Christ. Some tools of salvation cause us to grow spiritually and strengthen our ability to walk in the Spirit. Some are more mysterious, such as the nine gifts of the Holy Spirit, to whom we can submit, thereby allowing Him to flow through us (see 1 Corinthians 12:7–11). In addition, God gives some gifts, such as individual talents and traits, to all His created children. We bring these gifts with us into the body of Christ when we become Christians. They are part of our individual spirit. As part of spiritual worship, we may give them up to the Lord for His use and to His glory. The armor of God is one more set of gifts given to us so that we can be victorious and remain protected as we live in this world. This spiritual armor consists of the buckle of truth, the breastplate of righteousness, feet fitted with the gospel of peace, the shield of faith, the helmet of salvation, and the sword of the Spirit, which is the Word of God.

If I had clearly understood the certainty of my salvation in Christ before I plunged into spiritual battle, I would not have been such an easy target for the lies that Satan hurled at me. As I walked through that awful time, I learned to put on the whole armor of God. My favorite piece of the armor is the helmet of salvation because it protects the mind, and the mind is where many of our battles are fought. Once I knew the truth, that we are saved by the righteousness of Christ alone, and once the truth was confirmed to me in God's Word, my faith grew. It was then that the helmet of salvation was placed on my head and I began to live in the peace that can come only by knowing the certainty of salvation in Jesus.

CHAPTER 15

MY ADVENTURES IN THE SCRIPTURES

(Relevant Scripture: John 6:66–69)

My experiences with the Holy Bible have been both turbulent and glorious. If you recall, it was while reading the Scriptures that I received the final blow that sent me reeling into the depths of mental and spiritual turmoil. Nevertheless, it was also through reading the Holy Scriptures that I found many of the solutions to my mental and spiritual problems, making the Bible an essential part of my healing. My adventure into the Scriptures has been a wonderful mix of discovery, awe, and pure delight, along with more than a little confusion and frustration. I will be forever grateful to God the Father, God the Son, and God the Holy Spirit for their love, patience, and willingness to persevere with me. God has promised that if we seek Him with our whole heart, we will find Him. He has kept that promise to me, saving my life and my sanity in the process.

After that initial blow, my first instinct was to leave Bible study to the experts. I had to muster the courage to open the Bible again and begin to seek the answers I needed. There came a time during Jesus' ministry when some of His followers left Him. When Jesus turned to His twelve disciples, He asked, "You do not want to leave too, do you?" Simon Peter replied, "Lord to whom shall we go? You have the words of eternal life. We believe and know you are the Holy One of God" (John 6:67, 68). Simon Peter's answer exactly describes the place in which I found myself. There was no place for me to go. I knew that only God had the answers to my mental and spiritual problems, so I went to Him and to His written Word, the Holy Bible.

When I began my adventures into the Scriptures, the first change I noticed was that I had a great passion to read and understand them. I did not study the Scriptures in a methodical way, nor did I go for any formal education. What I did was simply seek the Lord, request the answers to my questions through prayer, spent time with other believers, and read the Bible. In the beginning, I spent most of my time in the Old Testament, which surprised me. However, the Old Testament stories began to change my perceptions about God. I came to know Him on a different level. One of the most fun and, at the same time, most frustrating things for me was that the Holy Spirit did not answer questions in the order in which I asked them. Instead, my understanding came in seemingly random ways, over many years, and not always in ways I expected. The Scriptures certainly became more alive to me, but, often, understanding would come to me simply. Someone would unknowingly say something that would cause a puzzle piece to fall into place, or I would suddenly have one of those light-bulb moments followed by a new revelation. It seemed to me that His Word was alive and came at me from all directions. One time, He even gave me an insight about His power through a pine-cleaner commercial! As time went on, I became more and more aware that the Holy Spirit was leading me and teaching me as I studied His written Word.

I also had experiences that were like seeing through the lens of a camera. They were like a snapshot of knowledge, but not the entire picture. These revelations would last for only as long as it took for a shutter to open and close. I labeled these revelations as "shutter experiences." These experiences imparted seeds of knowledge that continued to grow and that deepened my understanding over time. I will provide examples.

One evening, as I was mindlessly listening to the news, I heard a story about a divorce settlement between an athletic superstar and his wife. The judgment favored the athlete. According to the reporter, at the end of the proceeding, the judge asked for the athlete's autograph. In a split second, I experienced the Lord's offense about the injustice that had occurred in that courtroom. However, the offense went deeper and included the many injustices that had been committed against women over the course of time. It was an unexpected revelation, one I had not consciously sought to know. Today, I understand much more clearly God's plan and love for women in His Church and the world. God made woman an equal and powerful partner of Adam. Her authority reaches into all areas of life. Man and woman are created in the very image of God, and it takes both of them to make a complete image of Him. When we bar men or women from any segment of life in the Church, the family, or the world, we leave out one-half of the image of God. Our perspective narrows and the situation becomes out of balance as a result.

The most puzzling example of a revelation I received is the one I shared about the third area of the spiritual realm. I call it a theory because I cannot entirely confirm it by way of the Scriptures. My knowledge began with a shutter experience and developed over many years. It was Easter time and I was reading the account of Jesus' death and resurrection when I suddenly gleaned that there was something the Holy Spirit wanted me to understand about the time between Jesus' death and His resurrection. I knew it had to do with a time of transition after the death of the body, but that was all. The idea simmered on the back burner of my mind for years. Every once in a while, it would come to the forefront of my mind and I would get another clue. My understanding gradually deepened until; finally, the full understanding came. It was as if a large puzzle piece fell into place.

The Holy Bible
(Relevant Scriptures: 1 Corinthians 2:6–16;
John 14:25–26; Acts 17:11)

The Word of God is the knowledge, wisdom, will, and nature of the great I Am, or, put another way, the Word is God. The Word is manifested in the natural-realm world in three different ways by the triune God. It was through the spoken Word of God the Father that He created this natural-realm world. It was through creation that He began to make the invisible Word visible, for all creation witnesses the reality of God's existence. The realm of the unseen spiritual world is made visible, as this created world is patterned after the spiritual-realm world. God the Son was made visible through His embodiment in the flesh when He lived among us. It is through Jesus, the Word made flesh, that salvation is made available to all humankind. God the Holy Spirit made the invisible Word visible through the formation of the Holy Bible. This natural-realm tool enables us to grasp spiritual-realm truth in a way that can be comprehended by mere mortals. The Holy Bible is not God, nor is it magic. However, in the hands of the Holy Spirit, it becomes the living, powerful, and supernatural Word that can reach into the very depths of the soul and speak directly to the human spirit within us.

At first glance, the Holy Bible appears to be like any other book. It contains printed words on modern paper, bound together between a cover of one type or another.

Although it looks like a single book, it is really a collection of many written works that were created over a span of hundreds of years. These ancient writings were penned by many individuals, most of whom could not possibly have been in contact with one another. Much time and energy has been devoted to determining who wrote what and when they wrote it. The truth is, the Holy Bible has only one true author—and that is the Holy Spirit Himself. He is the one common denominator that links all the writers of Scripture, spanning the many years it took to pen them. When something is holy it is sacred and consecrated for a certain purpose. Indeed, the Holy Bible is just that, the written Word, set apart from every other written word, to be used by God the Holy Spirit to minister to us on all levels of our being.

This magnificent gift to the world is, without question, the most read and studied book in the history of the world. It has been read, dissected, understood, and misunderstood, sparking all kinds of arguments, controversies, and doctrines. The one thing it is not is benign. Like all things that have the power to reach into the spiritual-realm world, exposing the mind and ways of God, it is difficult for us to comprehend with the natural mind and intellect. The amazing thing about the Bible is not the written Word itself, but the fact that the Holy Spirit uses and anoints it to enlighten, encourage, discipline, and teach His people and the world the truth. This transforms the Scriptures into a living Word that makes it possible to study under the anointing of its eternal author. Just think, no matter what time in history you live, it is possible to study the Scriptures under the anointing of the Holy Spirit.

The Sword of the Spirit
(Relevant Scriptures: Hebrews 4:12; Ephesians 6:17; 2 Peter 1:20–21; 2 Timothy 3:15–17; Colossians 3:16)

Hebrews 4:12 tells us that the Word of God is living, active, and sharper than a double-edged sword. A two-edged sword is a weapon or tool used for thrusting or piercing. The Holy Scriptures are indeed the visible natural-realm tool the Holy Spirit uses to help accomplish His work of drawing all people to Christ. It also plays a major part in His ministry of sanctification in those who have already received Christ as their Savior. This powerful tool known as the sword of the spirit has a double edge that cuts on both sides. In the hands of the Holy Spirit, this mighty weapon brings life and death—life to the soul and spirit, and death to the sinful nature within us. In other words, it is instrumental in developing our spiritual life in God as well as in freeing us from the bondage of sin.

The Holy Spirit uses the Bible in so many ways that it is difficult to for me list them. It is through this one tool that He reveals the very nature and will of God so that we may seek Him and come to know Him. These words make known the wrath of God as well as the love of God, the judgment of God, and the forgiveness of God. It gives us God's uncompromising law and then applies His all-sufficient grace. The Holy Spirit uses His written Word to instruct us, to convict us of sin, and to comfort us when we have repented of our sin. These same Scriptures show us our need for salvation, and then lead us to the one true Savior. Once we are saved, these same words become a means of promoting our spiritual growth and intimacy with God, leading us into right living. The Holy Spirit also uses these powerful words to expose that which is hidden in darkness to teach about the true source of darkness, Satan himself. It is miraculous what can be accomplished in an individual who is willing to take to heart the sacred words found between the covers of the Holy Bible. When these words are properly understood and appropriately applied, they truly are God's Word of Life.

Keys to Understanding
(Relevant Scriptures: Ephesians 1:17; Luke 24:44–49)

In an attempt to help me understand what had happened to me on the night I read about the unpardonable sin, my pastor made this statement: "The trouble with the Bible is that it is so open to everyone." At the time, I didn't understand what he was telling me, but, as my understanding grew, I saw the truth in what he said. Unfortunately, the Scriptures can also be misinterpreted and abused, leading to wrong application and confusion. My personal experience with the Scriptures is a testimony to this very real problem. To begin with, when we read and study the Scriptures, we bring with us all our fears, questions, preconceived ideas, experiences, personalities, and intellect. All these things can keep us, at least for a time, from having a balanced approach to the Bible. For example, if we are legalistic in our thinking, then we read the Scriptures through the prism of legalism. This causes an unbalanced focus on the law. If we are skeptical and unbelieving, then this is the mind-set we have as we begin to study the Scriptures.

To rightly understand and apply the Scriptures, there are some key things we need to understand. I call them the keys to understanding. As important as these keys are to studying the Scriptures, the most essential key is that we seek an active relationship with the Holy Spirit, asking Him to lead us as we study His written Word. He has blessed the people of His Church with a variety of ways to begin our studies. Three of the nine gifts of the Holy Spirit have to do with knowledge. They are the gifts of knowledge, wisdom, and discernment. These supernatural gifts are available to believers through the Holy Spirit, who is part of the learning experience. He has also blessed the Church with teachers who have been anointed to teach and preach the Scriptures in their proper application, helping us to gain understanding and direction. However, since we are all humans, even the anointed teachers can make mistakes, so the Holy Spirit also gives us His gift of discernment to help us determine if Scripture is being misused or inappropriately applied. Bible study is part of our walk in the Spirit; because of this, it is a process of learning as we grow in our knowledge of God and His written Word.

Word Logo and Word Rhema
(Relevant Scriptures: John 1:1–5, 14; Jeremiah 33:3)

Early in my great adventure into the Scriptures, I had a moment of revelation that is as precious to me today as it was thirty-plus years ago. I was reading in the Old Testament when I came upon a verse that spoke to me in a way that I had not yet experienced. It was as if the verse had been written especially for me and God was using it to speak directly to me. It read, "Call on me and I will answer you and tell you great and unsearchable things you do not know" (Jeremiah 33:3). There is no way I can describe how I knew that the Holy Spirit was using that Scripture to speak personally to me. All I can tell you is that I knew it without a doubt—and I was thrilled. The woman with all the nagging questions, the one who believed but also longed to understand, the one who was in mental and spiritual turmoil, was going to get answers to her questions from the only One who could answer them. My understanding of how God used this verse to speak to me became my first key as to how the Holy Spirit uses His written Word.

What I later learned about this experience is the difference between word logo and word rhema. Logo is the entire written Word of God given to all of us. The Holy Spirit gives us knowledge, wisdom, and revelations regarding the Scriptures for the purposes of our spiritual growth and understanding. Rhema is when the Holy Spirit uses the written Word to speak specifically to an individual at a certain moment in time. In other words, He inspires the reader in such a way that he or she understands that the message was sent directly to him or her at that time and for a specific reason. I have received both types of revelation many times in the years after that first time. Through word logo, I have learned to understand and appreciate many Bible lessons and stories, which has enabled me to implement them in my life and deepen my faith. I have experienced word rhema less often, but when I have, it was usually a confirmation of truth or a direction that I had been seeking. However, it is important to understand that rhema is always accompanied by a knowing supernatural faith and is not something you can manifest on your own. Both logo and rhema are wonderful and important ways in which the Holy Spirit uses the written Word to communicate with us.

Who, What, Where, and When

One of the most basic keys to Bible study is that Scripture should be read in the context of when it was given. It always has to be put in the context of the entire Scriptures. In other words, it is important to ask, like any good detective or reporter, the questions of who, what, where, and when. It is necessary to ask who is speaking and to whom the person is speaking (e.g., to believers or unbelievers). What is the situation and what is the writer trying to convey? When did this take place? Was it before Christ, during Jesus' life on Earth, or after His resurrection? When we don't place the Scriptures into their proper context, we greatly increase our chances of misunderstanding their true meaning and put ourselves at risk of starting doctrines and practices that are out of balance and incomplete.

The Bible is basically set up in three categories. The Old Testament records the history of God's interaction with us before Jesus' birth. The Gospels are the first four books of the New Testament. They record the birth, life, death, and resurrection of Jesus, as well His ministry on Earth. The Epistles make up the third section and record the formation and history of the early Church. They begin with the book of Acts, which records the coming of the Holy Spirit at Pentecost, and end with the book of Revelation.

Eternal Life and Kingdom Living

Early in my Bible reading, I had a tendency to attach all Scripture to eternal life in Jesus. In other words, I wanted to know what was required to accept and keep my eternal destination in God's heavenly kingdom. Then, in one of those snapshot moments, I received the understanding that eternal life in Christ and the principles of living in His kingdom are two different things. Eternal-life Scriptures apply to the first stage of salvation, wherein we accept Jesus as our Savior. Kingdom-living Scriptures give us insight into the kingdom of God and the principles of living that are part of His kingdom. Once we have accepted Christ, the kingdom-living Scriptures are applied to the second stage of salvation. In other words, they show us how to live in the salvation we already have in Jesus.

When we read and apply the Scriptures before we have accepted Jesus, they all work together to show our need to accept Jesus as our Savior. They inform us of our sinful condition and illustrate the impossibility of perfectly following God's laws. They also expose God's holiness, leading us to accept Jesus and enter into God's spiritual kingdom. Once we have accepted Jesus, we are a citizen of His kingdom and begin to learn and live under the principles of that kingdom. Sometimes, unfortunately, Christians don't completely make that transition and continue attaching salvation in Christ to the kingdom-living principles. When we do this, it will not be long before we become uncertain about our eternal destination—and so we begin working for the salvation in Christ that we already possess.

Connie Becker

The Three Levels of the Holy Bible

Hebrews 4:12 informs us that the Word of God penetrates and even divides soul and spirit and joints and marrow. We are three-part people. The Holy Scriptures are designed to minister to us on all three levels of our existence. It is because we consist of a soul and a spirit housed in a body that the Holy Bible has three distinct layers contained in it. When we are able to approach the Bible knowing that these layers exist within the Scriptures, we become less confused about how properly to apply these powerful written words.

The Physical Level

The body is what defines us as citizens of this natural, created world. The first level of Scripture deals directly with the natural-realm world and our physical life on Earth. This level is perhaps the easiest for us to comprehend because we can study it and approach it in the same way we would any other teaching. It is on this level that the Bible is very much a history book, revealing God's interaction with His created world and its citizens.

The Bible begins with the creation of the world and progresses through the fall of humanity and the history of God's dealings with the fallen world. The words of the ancient prophets of God are recorded within the pages of Scripture as His plan of salvation is revealed. The

Bible continues to document the birth, life, death, and resurrection of Jesus. It chronicles the powerful happenings that followed the event of Pentecost, when the Holy Spirit was released to dwell within the hearts and spirits of all believers in Christ Jesus. It also provides the history of the early Church. It ends with foretelling the ultimate future of this created realm as it passes away and a new heaven and a new Earth emerge. On this level, we are able to comprehend the events of the past. At the same time, the Bible prepares us for what the future holds for Earth and its inhabitants.

It is on the physical level of Scripture that we begin to intellectually understand who God is, who we are, and our sinful condition, as well as His ultimate will for us. The process of accepting or rejecting God's plan of salvation begins here as people are introduced to Christ Jesus.

The Level of the Soul

The soul is where our psychological nature is housed. The Holy Bible is the most powerful psychology book ever written. The second level of Scripture targets the deeper recesses of the soul, reaching into the heart, which is the control center of one's being. It is in the soul that we suffer some of the most painful ramifications of sin. Our bodies can fall ill or be damaged simply by living in this sinful atmosphere. However, it is the turmoil and distress harbored in the soul and spirit that can cause the body, soul, and spirit to become ill and broken. It is on this level that we receive the information about the care of the soul and the needs of the spirit. We learn the importance of seeking God and establishing a relationship with Him. It is through this level of Scripture that we receive the tools of Communion, and confession of sin, as well as forgiveness and prayer. When we practice these powerful gifts, they minister to our souls and spirits and free our minds of the burdens of sin. They also strengthen our faith and our relationship with the Lord.

This level is also used to touch the soul and spirit on a deeper level. The human heart contains chambers that store painful memories and damage done to us by our own sin, by the sin of others, and by living in this fallen world. This hidden damage deep in the soul is often the source of unwanted attitudes and behaviors. The Holy Spirit uses the second level of Scripture to minister to the dark, damaged chambers of the soul. However, we must invite Him to do so and be willing to open the door so He may heal us.

I had spent so many years stuffing things I couldn't deal with deep into my mind that many of my chambers needed to be cleansed and healed. I call this process "closet cleaning" because that is exactly how it works. If you have ever cleaned a closet, then you know what a mess you can create in the process. Everything hidden behind a door is now all over the room, and you are not sure what to do with it. The cleansing of the soul is no different. I started the process by asking the Holy Spirit to heal my soul and spirit. As humans, we have a tendency to want to hide things from God and sometimes from ourselves, so my process began when I became honest with myself and God. One by one, many of those dark chambers in my heart were opened. I got better and better until my heart was full of freedom and joy. One of the many things I learned during this process is never to run from God's judgment. Always run toward it, for His judgment holds within it His love and forgiveness, which brings about one's freedom. The truth definitely does set us free.

The Level of the Spirit

The level of the spirit is the deepest and most enlightening of the three levels of the Holy Bible because it is revealed only by the Holy Spirit. It is true that the Holy Spirit gives us revelations so we may understand all levels of Scripture; however, the deeper, spiritual level of the Scriptures can only be seen if the Holy Spirit reveals it. In ancient times, the scribes knew about this level and would pore over the Scriptures in a search to discover the deeper meanings contained in the Scriptures. There is much discussion, especially concerning the Old Testament, as to whether some of the stories actually happened or if they are allegorical. I personally believe that they are both. Early in my studies of the Scriptures, I asked what I call either–or questions. Then one day, the Holy Spirit broke into my thoughts with this understanding: "Sometimes it can be both."

Once the Holy Spirit reveals to us the deeper meaning in the Scriptures, we can convey it to others. It is most likely that many of the Church's doctrines and practices were understood and put into practice because the Holy Spirit revealed a deep spiritual meaning to an anointed priest or teacher. I believe it likely that this is how the different denominations within the Church came into being. The Holy Spirit revealed a truth; some Christians implemented it, and others did not. This is how the Church grows in its understanding. This is also where we must use the Holy Spirit's gift of discernment to determine what is from Him and what is not. I have come to a place where I can often discern the difference between those things the Holy Spirit has revealed to a teacher or preacher and those things the speaker has learned through traditional studies. Both are important and both are for our understanding, but they are received on a completely different level.

The Three Levels of the Ten Commandments

In closing this chapter, I provide a simple example of taking one section of Scripture and revealing the three levels contained within in it. The Ten Commandments show us how God uses His written Word to touch us on all three levels of our being.

The Physical Level

The Ten Commandments are the foundation for a civil society. God gave them to the Israelites so their way of living would stand out among all other nations. It is on the physical level that the Ten Commandments teach humankind how to live in relationship with God and each other forming a standard of right living. This is one important reason why we must teach our children the Ten Commandments. In modern society, some people are suffering because they have little knowledge of God's principles for right living laid out in the Ten Commandments.

The Level of the Soul

On this level, the Ten Commandments are God's standard of righteousness. When we do not know what is righteous, we cannot know what is unrighteous. This level ministers to our soul and is a two-way mirror that reveals the righteousness of God as well as our own sinful condition. Sinful behavior causes distress and damage to our conscious mind and our deep mind. Knowledge of God's righteousness and the demands of His righteousness convict us of our sin and show us how to avoid harmful behaviors that can cause us emotional pain. This leads us to seek God and His plan of salvation.

Connie Becker

The Level of the Spirit

Earlier in this book, I shared my revelation about the spiritual level of the Ten Commandments, but, because it is a great example of the deeper spiritual meaning of the Scriptures, I repeat it here. It is typical of God to give us a task or instructions and then provide us with all we need to carry it out. Once we accept Jesus as our Savior, we become His children of salvation and are saved by His righteousness. It is then that, for believers only, the Ten Commandments are transformed into His ten promises. As we proceed on our journey to become like Christ, we are promised that, one day, we shall be able to obey God's commandments. This promise will not be completely fulfilled until we leave the body, and the sinful nature along with it, behind. Until then, the Ten Commandments remain our standard of right living, defining the parameters for our way of life. They continue to be a mirror that reveals our sinfulness, but for those who have accepted Jesus, they have also become His ten promises. We can look forward to the time when we will be able to obey God, starting with practicing the greatest commandment of all, that we "Love the Lord your God with all your heart and with all your soul and with all your mind."(Matthew 22:37)

In many ways, the Holy Bible is like a manufacturer's handbook meant to benefit us as we live in this natural-realm world. It also prepares us for life in the spiritual realm. It is very much like the thick book we receive when we buy a new car. Many times, I have left that book in its wrapper, tucked in the glove compartment. In so doing, I have missed out on understanding how to use some of the car's gizmos and gadgets. I usually open the owners' manual only if I'm having some kind of problem with the car; then, I am shocked to learn how much information is available to me. It is even more amazing what we can learn from our Creator when we open and read the Holy Bible.

CHAPTER 16

CAN A CHRISTIAN LOSE HIS OR HER SALVATION?

The question that most haunted me, the one I most wanted answered was, Can a Christian lose his or her salvation? This question is a source of disagreement among the different denominations of the Church. The doctrines of some denominations teach that a Christian can renounce his or her belief in Christ Jesus, while others are equally adamant that once a person has accepted Jesus as Savior, it is impossible to lose salvation. This is an age-old dispute that I cannot hope to settle. Nevertheless, I will say this: No matter what you believe, you are left with the need to reconcile conflicting Scriptures that validate the opposite belief. These seemingly contradictory Scriptures caused me the most difficulty in my quest to answer this question for myself. I went directly to the Lord with my predicament.

Slowly, over many years, He convinced me that He will never let go of anyone who has accepted Him as Savior.

Dealing with Conflicting Scriptures
(Relevant Scripture: Luke 4:1–13)

One intriguing aspect of the Bible is that it is a mighty weapon that we can use in spiritual warfare. It was when absolute chaos broke loose in my mind that I first became aware of spiritual warfare. Most of the time, we are not consciously aware that a spiritual war is being waged. There is—and this has been the case since Lucifer fell. It took me a while to finally accept the fact that it was Satan, the Enemy of my soul, who was the source of the horrible thought-attacks against God that were happening in my head. At the time, I didn't even believe that Satan existed. I had fallen into the trap of believing that he was just a symbol standing for the existence of evil. Or, perhaps, Satan was an excuse for people's sinful behavior.

It was when the Holy Spirit gave me the first weapon to use in my plight that I began to learn what a mighty weapon the Scriptures are in spiritual battle. In addition to supplying me with the keys to understanding the Scriptures (which I shared in chapter fifteen), the Holy Spirit taught me other important lessons about how to apply the Scriptures. These are especially helpful when I am dealing with seemingly conflicting Scriptures or when the Enemy of my soul is using Scripture to attack and deceive me.

One of these lessons came to me as I was struggling over the meaning of a certain Scripture. I was running an errand in a large department store when, in frustration, I accidently spoke aloud the dialogue that was taking place in my mind. Right in the middle of the store, I said, "Well, if this Scripture doesn't mean you can lose your salvation, then what does it mean?" I got an immediate revelation that day; however, it was in the form of another question: If you are going to understand the purpose of this Scripture as confirmation that a Christian can lose his or her salvation, then what are you going to do with the Scriptures that say the opposite? This didn't answer the question I had asked, but it did give me the beginning of new insight on how to apply Scripture. The way Jesus handled the Scriptures when He was tempted by Satan gave me further understanding of what the Holy Spirit was trying to teach me.

Jesus answered Satan's temptations with the proper application of Scripture. As an example, when Satan took Jesus to the top of the highest steeple, he used this Scripture to tempt Jesus: "If you are the Son of God, throw yourself down. For it is written 'He will command his angels concerning you, to guard you carefully, they will lift you up in their hands so that you will not strike your foot against a stone.'" Jesus answered, "It says: 'Do not put the

Lord your God to the test.'" (Luke 4:9-12) In doing this, Jesus put the meanings of the two Scriptures in their proper balance, thereby clarifying their purpose.

The purpose of the first Scripture was not to give Jesus permission to throw himself off of high places in some spectacular display of His deity. Nor did it mean that Jesus would never suffer harm in this world. Instead, the purpose was to reveal the care that God the Father had for His Son and to confirm that the spiritual realm's angels were tending to His needs. What is fascinating to me about this exchange is that Jesus didn't try to explain to Satan his misrepresentation of the Scripture; instead, Jesus simply applied another Scripture to the first one. This exchange between Satan and Jesus shows us two things: Scripture can be used as a weapon against the tricks of Satan, and the balanced meaning of Scripture can be found by applying one Scripture's meaning to that of another. It also shows that Satan will use Scripture against us if we let him. This knowledge became a valuable tool in my spiritual battle. Whenever the thought-attacks came upon me, trying to convince me that I had lost my salvation in Jesus, I simply answered with a conflicting Scripture.

My first lesson about how to use Scripture in spiritual battle came to me at the very beginning of my mental and physical turmoil. Satan was using the Scripture of the "unpardonable sin" to badger me, lie to me, and horrify me. He was trying to destroy me, and I had no defense against Him. Then one day, the Holy Spirit broke into the turmoil of my mind, instructing me to answer those thought-attacks with these words: "Contrary to the Word of God." I did my best to obey Him; however, the one thing I could not understand was why the Scripture about the "unpardonable sin" was contrary to the Word of God, given that it was certainly part of God's written Word. It took me a while to realize that it was not the Scripture that was contrary to God's Word; it was the application of the Scripture.

The improper application of scripture is a common trick used by Satan to horrify a believer and destroy the knowledge of his or her security in Christ. Sometimes, he is less overt and not as destructive as he was in my life. Many times, he covertly plants only enough doubt to make the believer uncertain of his or her salvation in Christ and stunt that person's spiritual growth. It is not uncommon for pastors to receive visits from believers who are distressed about the Scripture discussing the unpardonable sin. When I experienced this kind of attack from Satan, it was as if I had been shot with a gun. Fear and horror spread through my soul and it was all a misinterpretation of scripture that Satan was using to destroy my faith. So, hoping to spare someone else from taking this route, I will share what I know to be the truth.

Connie Becker

The Unpardonable Sin
(Relevant Scriptures: Mark 3:20–30; John 3:16–21, 31)

The Scripture about unpardonable sin, also called the blasphemy of the Holy Spirit, reads as follows (initially, Jesus is speaking): "'I tell you the truth, all sins and blasphemies of men will be forgiven them. But whoever blasphemes against the Holy Spirit will never be forgiven; he is guilty of eternal sin.' He said this because they were saying, 'He had an evil spirit'" (Mark 3:28–30). As we explore the meaning of this Scripture, we must first put it in the context of when and to whom Jesus spoke the words. To begin with, Jesus made this statement before His death and resurrection. The unpardonable sin comes under the umbrella of "everything changes" after Jesus' death and resurrection. When Jesus died on the cross, He died for all sin. Therefore, the unpardonable sin can no longer be committed in the same way it was before His death and resurrection. In other words, there is no longer a sin that God won't forgive if one recognizes his or her sin and comes to Him for forgiveness.

I found the following statement in the devotional magazine *In Touch* of August 2003.

> The unpardonable sin was an offense committed by those who witnessed the indisputable, irrefutable evidence that Jesus was who He claimed to be. Though the Jewish leaders saw the work of the Holy Spirit through the incarnate

Jesus Christ, they attributed the work to Satan; Jesus said this was unforgivable because they deliberately denied the clear proof of His deity. Regrettably, this passage has too often been scrutinized outside of its original context. Instead of building a belief system on a single statement, we should exercise diligence to discover what the Bible as a whole says about forgiveness. John informs us that there is absolutely no sin that Christ will not forgive—not a single transgression from which He will not cleanse us—if only we will agree with God that our wrongdoing is sin.

Warren W. Wiersbe explains it this way: "People today cannot commit the 'unpardonable sin' in the same way the Jewish religious leaders did when Jesus was ministering on earth. The only sin today that God cannot forgive is rejection of his Son." (The Bible Exposition Commentary) In other words, it is the Holy Spirit who convicts us of sin, reveals the truth about Jesus, and woos us to accept Jesus as our Savior. When we resist the Holy Spirit and do not believe Him that Jesus is the Savior of the world, we commit the unpardonable sin. However, it is only unforgivable until the moment we believe the Holy Spirit and ask Jesus to be our Savior. The deliberate denial and rejection of Jesus is the only unpardonable sin. This is because Jesus is the only means of salvation. For those who have accepted Jesus as their Savior, there is no such thing as a sin that He can't or won't forgive.

Connie Becker

Is It Possible for a Christian to Turn Away from God?
(Relevant Scriptures: Colossians 2:9–11; Romans 8:1–2)

Another line of reasoning is that a Christian can simply change his or her mind and recant his or her acceptance of Jesus as Savior. The thinking here is that God gave us free will and we can exercise that free will to disavow our belief in Jesus any time we choose. It is true that, as we learn about salvation in Jesus, we can go through a time of indecision. During this time, we can bounce back and forth between deciding to accept Jesus or not. However, once you have accepted Him and His sacrifice for your sin, you have accepted the very Way of salvation. You cannot recant that decision or turn away from it, for you have been made one with the Spirit of God and have become His child of salvation. The decision to believe and accept Jesus is not simply a whim of your conscious mind. It is the combination of your conscious mind, your deep mind (the heart), and your individual spirit, together making a collective decision in favor of Christ. This makes the decision irrevocable because, of your own free will, you have made the choice that is confirmed by your conscious mind, your heart, and your spirit.

The Lord made this truth clear to me during a particularly difficult time in my long struggle to trust Him. A time came when I wanted to quit. It was all too hard and I wanted to go back. I received a vision of myself climbing a mountain. I was in a crevice so tight that I could barely move. I tried to turn around and was simply unable to. There was only one way I could go, and that was forward. I have come to understand that once a person has truly accepted Jesus as Savior, he or she has made an irrevocable decision for Christ and has given him- or herself to His everlasting care and protection. He will never let go of you. He will never leave you.

It has taken me many years to grasp how great and powerful a salvation we actually have in Jesus. I went through times when I had trouble understanding exactly what the difference was between before and after one accepts Jesus. It seemed to me that there were still all kinds of rules and situations that could cause me to be separated from Christ. I now know that I simply misunderstood Scripture or wrongly applied it. I cannot recall a biblical account where a person actually went on to lose salvation in Christ Jesus after accepting Him once He was resurrected. But I have heard people provide three different examples as proof that a Christian can lose his or her salvation. These examples are Lucifer, Ananias and Sapphira, and Judas.

Lucifer

Some cite Lucifer's and his followers' spiritual-realm rebellion as proof that we can turn away from God after we have been born again. However, this example does not prove that it is possible to reject Christ once we have accepted His salvation, because Satan's rebellion against God happened in the spiritual realm long before Jesus' sacrifice. Everything changed after Christ lived, died, and was resurrected. This is true in the natural-realm world as well as in the spiritual-realm world. The change is for all eternity.

Ananias and Sapphira
(Relevant Scripture: Acts 5:1–11)

The story of Ananias and Sapphira tells that they were struck dead at the altar because they lied to the church about their offering. However, theirs was a physical death, not necessarily a spiritual death that caused them to lose their eternal salvation. The story indicates that God took them out of this world and dealt with their actions in the spiritual realm. We must remember that this happened during the early stages of the Church when many new things— all of them strange to the new believers—were put into practice. God was most likely teaching Ananias and Sapphira strong lessons, just as He did with the Israelites in the desert. Just because God took them out of this world does not mean that He banished them from heaven. If they were true believers, they had the covering of Christ Jesus and God was simply disciplining His children of salvation. They lost their life on Earth, probably for the sake of the new Church.

Judas

(Relevant Scriptures: Matthew 26:14–16, 27:3–5; John 13:18–30, 17:12)

Judas is another person who confounds us as we read the account of his actions. What could be worse than being the man who, after personally knowing Jesus, betrayed Him to His enemies for money? Judas was most likely among those who believed that the Savior would come and rescue them from the political circumstances of the time. When he realized the ramifications of his actions, he was devastated and tried to return the money he had received. He was so remorseful that he took his own life. I am not trying to defend Judas in any way, but I am saying that we must look at the Scripture in context. To begin with, Judas' actions took place before Jesus died and was resurrected. At that time, no believer had the Holy Spirit living within their heart because the covering for sin had not yet been provided. The Holy Spirit did not dwell within believers until the day of Pentecost, which was after the resurrection of Jesus.

This means that Judas came under the same conditions as did all other spiritual-realm citizens waiting in Paradise for the resurrection of the Lord. I am not making any judgments about Judas' eternal destination. I am saying that the possibility exists that he was given an opportunity to repent, confess, and accept the sacrifice of Christ for his sins. Only God would know if Judas had irrevocably rejected His plan of salvation. If that is what Judas did, then I know that Judas was put in this position because God foreknew that he would never accept Jesus as his Savior. However, the way that Judas behaved when he realized the ramifications of his actions does suggest that he was repentant and remorseful for what he had done. It is possible; when Jesus made the statement that he lost only one disciple that He was referring only in the context of this natural-realm world.

Summary

When I study the Scriptures in detail, as I have been doing for years, I learn the importance of applying the keys to understanding if I want to truly discern their meaning. The questions of who, what, when, and where are important, along with the knowledge of the two stages of salvation and the three levels of the Scriptures. This is especially important when reading the letters to the early churches. In those letters, the apostles deal with the newness of the Christian faith and the radical changes it brought about for Jewish believers and Gentiles alike. We must keep in mind that many times, when a disciple is speaking to early believers, he knows that he is building on a foundation of knowledge already understood by those to whom he is speaking. In other words, it was not important to teach people that their eternal salvation was secure in Christ because they already had that information. The disciples are speaking of the second stage of salvation, which is living in the salvation they already possess. Many times, the writers of epistles are trying to convince people to let go of old rituals, practices, and idols they worshiped in the past. They are attempting to teach the new Christians that Christ's sacrifice provides all that is needed for their salvation. There is nothing that can be added to it, nor is there anything we can do to destroy it.

Christians may suffer many ramifications when they do not stand on the solid foundation of what Jesus accomplished on the cross. However, a shaky foundation cannot cause them to lose their salvation. Still, it can certainly make them doubt their security in Jesus as well as the security of their eternal destination. When we begin to add things we must do to be saved, we water down Jesus' sacrifice and start focusing on what we do instead of on who He is and what He has done. This practice weakens our faith, retards our spiritual growth, and affects our relationship with the Lord.

As we live out our salvation, our actions are important and have ramifications, both positive and negative, in this world and in the spiritual realm alike, but they do not alter in any way Jesus' sacrifice for the salvation of our souls or our eternal destination in Him. I have suffered much turmoil, not because I was not saved or had committed some unforgivable sin, but because of my lack of understanding of the security I have in Christ. I was not depending on the awesome power of Christ's sacrifice alone. Failing to do this can rob a believer of the peace on Earth that Jesus died to give us.

In addition to all the wonderful things the Lord has taught me on my journey with Him, two deciding factors finally convinced me that a Christian cannot lose his or her salvation in Christ. The first one is a matter of focus. The belief that we can lose our salvation focuses on our own actions and what we do. This puts the power of salvation in a human being's weak, incapable hands, which makes salvation only as strong as the individual is. The belief that a Christian cannot lose their salvation focuses on what Jesus did and validates the power of what He accomplished on the cross. It also confirms the promises Jesus made to all those who accept Him as their Savior. Jesus did not come to give us a second chance; He came to give us a second choice. When we choose to accept salvation through Jesus, it is a permanent choice that entirely depends on the power of what Jesus did on the cross. The second deciding factor came to me through another beautiful revelation regarding the inheritance of the second birth. I have held this revelation close to my heart for many years. I explain it in detail in the next chapter.

CHAPTER 17

THE INHERITANCE OF THE SECOND BIRTH

(Relevant Scriptures: Romans 9:6–13; Malachi 1:2–3)

As I struggled to understand the Scriptures that seemed to say a Christian could lose his or her salvation, I received the beginning of a revelation that, once complete, answered the question for me. I cannot think of this revelation without smiling, as it began with a Scripture that greatly disturbed me. I was reading Romans 9:10–13:

> Not only that, but Rebekah's children had one and the same father, our father Isaac. Yet before the twins were born or had done anything good or bad—in order that God's purpose in election might stand: not by works but by him who calls—she was told [by God], the older will serve

> the younger. Just as it is written: "Jacob I loved, but Esau I hated."

My first thought about this Scripture was, *If God hates certain people before they are even born, then how is it possible to know that I am not among those He hates?* This Scripture rocked my world for a while, but the revelations that followed built my trust, quieted my soul, and deepened my love for God beyond my ability to describe. The revelation I received began with the above Scripture and continued to include five more Scriptures, mostly from the Old Testament. The Old Testament accounts include those of Cain and Abel, Ishmael and Isaac, Esau and Jacob, Moses and Joshua, and Saul and David—and end with Adam and Jesus. Many important lessons are taught using the example of the lives of these people. However, the revelation I received is on the level of the Spirit and revealed a pattern of a deep spiritual truth that confirmed for me the security of our salvation in Christ through the inheritance of the second birth.

Esau and Jacob
(Relevant Scripture: Genesis 25:19–34)

Esau and Jacob were the twin sons of Isaac and Rebekah. The twins were at odds with each other even in their mother's womb. They jostled so much inside her that

Rebekah asked the Lord what was happening to her. "The Lord said to her, 'Two nations are in your womb, and two peoples from within you will be separated; one people will be stronger than the other, and the older will serve the younger.'" (Genesis 25:22-23) The twins were very different. Esau grew up to be a skilled hunter and loved the open country, while Jacob was a quiet man who spent his time among the tents. One day, as Jacob was sitting near the fire cooking some stew, Esau returned famished and tired from a hunting trip. He asked Jacob for a bowl of stew. Jacob replied, "First sell me your birthright." "Look I am about to die," Esau said, "What good is my birthright if I am dead?" (Genesis 25: 31-32) Then he swore to Jacob that his brother could have his birthright in exchange for a bowl of stew. Esau was the firstborn of the twins, so his inheritance was that of the first son. Later, Jacob, with the help of Rebekah, his mother, also tricked Esau out of his father's blessing, meaning that Esau lost his father's blessing as well as his own birthright. In the end, Jacob, the second-born son, inherited everything that traditionally was the birthright of the firstborn son.

It is hard to condone the behaviors of Esau, Jacob, Isaac, and Rebekah in this story. As parents, Rebekah and Isaac each favored a son. Isaac favored Esau, and Rebekah favored Jacob. This alone caused rivalry between the siblings. Jacob took advantage of his brother and even deceived him to receive the blessing meant for Esau. Esau was rash and careless, treating his birthright as a cheap thing worth no more than a bowl of stew. I can understand how God would be displeased by both young men's behavior. However, it was only Esau whom God said He hated even before he was born. This means that God's hatred of Esau had nothing to do with what Esau had or had not done. God is making a statement about the deeper spiritual meaning of this Scripture.

What God is conveying through the story of Esau, the first born and Jacob, the second born twins is the difference between what we inherit through our first birth into this natural realm world and what we inherit when we are born again of God's Spirit. The sinful nature is the inheritance of our first birth into this world. Of course, God hated the sinful nature before it was ever born into humanity. It has caused nothing but pain, suffering, and, worst of all, separation from God. On the other hand, Jacob, the second-born twin, represents the inheritance of the second birth when we accept Jesus as our Savior and are born again of the Spirit of God. It is through the second, spiritual birth that we regain our inheritance in the kingdom of God and our spirits are reunited with God's Spirit.

We can glean other things from this story. God told Rebekah that two nations lived within her. One stood for the sinful nature that comes from Satan and is of his princedom. The other stands for the very Spirit of God and His heavenly kingdom. The twins jostled within their mother because they could not get along. In the same way, once we are born again of God's Spirit, we experience a tension between our born-again nature and the sinful nature that resides in us. There will always be enmity between the two until we leave our bodies and the sinful nature behind.

Two times, Jacob tricked Esau into giving up his firstborn's inheritance. At first glance, the tactics that Jacob used seem unfair. However, what Jacob was actually doing was reclaiming what was rightfully his in the first place, before Satan tricked Adam and Eve into eating the forbidden fruit. In the beginning, the human spirit was to have control over the soul and the body; however, when the sinful nature entered the heart of humankind, this was overturned. When we are born again of God's Spirit, we begin the process of reinstating the Spirit to its proper position. In other words, the second birth takes place after, not before, we are born into this world, which makes it the younger of the two births. The younger, spiritual birth is meant to control the firstborn nature as we live on Earth.

Esau's giving his birthright to Jacob presents an exact picture of what we do when we accept Jesus. The inheritance of the firstborn, sinful nature in us results in sin, death, and separation from God. The inheritance of our second birth results in the eventual freedom from sin, the death of the sinful nature, and everlasting spiritual life in God. When Esau gave up his birthright to Jacob, he unwittingly made an important statement: "What good is my birthright if I am dead?" The truth is, when we are born into this world, we are already dead to the Spirit of

God. We can inherit the world and all its treasures, but if we do not have our salvation in Christ Jesus, then we have nothing when we die. It is through the second birth that we inherit our eternal destination in the kingdom of God. The worth of this spiritual inheritance is far beyond our ability to calculate, for it is an eternal and everlasting inheritance.

Cain and Abel
(Relevant Scripture: Genesis 4)

Cain and Abel were the first two sons of Adam and Eve. Cain was the firstborn, and Abel was the second-born. Cain worked the soil and Abel kept flocks of sheep. When the time came for them to make an offering to the Lord, Cain brought fruits from the soil and Abel brought fat portions from some of the firstborn of his flock. God looked with favor on Abel and his offering, but He did not favor Cain and his offering.

Here again, the different levels of Scripture can be applied and different lessons of truth can be learned. The revelation I received concerns the offerings of Cain and Abel on the deeper spiritual level of the scriptures. Cain represents the first born sinful nature in all of us. Cain's offering was not accepted because God is revealing to us that there is no offering and nothing the sinful nature in us can do to atone for the sin manifested in that nature. The only offering that can atone for the firstborn nature in all of us is represented by the offering of the second-born son, Abel. Abel stands for our second, spiritual birth. His offering included the shedding of blood. The price of sin is death. When Jesus' body died and He shed His blood, He atoned for the sin of all humankind. We can receive this sacrifice only through our second, spiritual birth when we accept Jesus as our Savior.

Ishmael and Isaac

(Relevant Scriptures: Genesis 16, 18:1–15, 21:1–20; Romans 9:1–9)

Ishmael and Isaac are the two sons of Abraham. Abraham and his wife, Sarah, were unable to have children, even though God had promised Abraham that he would have a son from his own body. As the couple entered their old age still childless, they decided that Abraham should have a child with Sarah's maidservant, Hagar. In so doing, Abraham would have an heir from his own body, as God had promised. In other words, they did not wait for the child God had promised; instead, they took matters into their own hands. Abraham loved Ishmael, his firstborn son, but his birth created discord between Sarah and Hagar, causing strife in Abraham's household. It was when Abraham was a hundred years old and Sarah, well past her childbearing years, was ninety years old that she gave birth to the child God had promised her and Abraham. They named Abraham's second-born son Isaac.

Ishmael was born because Abraham and Sarah made a decision apart from the will of God. He was conceived under normal circumstances and because Abraham and Sarah did not wait for God's promise to become reality. In the same way, it was through Adam and Eve's decision to disregard God's instruction and eat the forbidden fruit that brought the sinful nature to reside in them. As a result, the sinful nature became the inheritance for all humanity. Isaac, on the other hand, was conceived by way of a miracle, through two individuals well past their childbearing years. Isaac was the child God had promised to both Abraham and Sarah. His birth was the result of the direct intervention of God. Isaac was the child of the promise of God, conceived through His supernatural intervention. Jesus, in the same way, is the promised Savior. He was also miraculously conceived by the direct intervention of God. Again in this story, Ishmael, the firstborn son, stands for our first birth into this natural-realm world. Isaac, the second-born son, stands for our second, spiritual birth when we are born again of God's Spirit.

Ishmael and Isaac represent two separate kingdoms and two different covenants of God. God's covenant with Ishmael, the firstborn, came in the form of a blessing. God promised that He would be with Ishmael and make for him a great nation, increasing his numbers. This promise given to Ishmael was of the natural-realm world and was only for the time Ishmael lived on Earth. And this is the same promise that God gives to all His children of creation when they are born into this world. The blessings and trials of this natural-realm world are the only inheritance we receive through our first birth. God's covenant with Isaac, the second-born, is an everlasting, eternal covenant with him and all his descendants. This is the inheritance we receive through our second, spiritual birth when we are born again of the Spirit of God in the moment we accept Jesus as our Savior. This is an eternal covenant that cannot be broken. Once we accept Jesus as our Savior, we are born again of incorruptible seed. This seed is eternal. It can neither die nor be broken because it is a result of the everlasting promise of God. It is through the second birth that the first birth is redeemed and saved.

Moses and Joshua
(Relevant Scriptures: Numbers 20:1–13; Deuteronomy 1:38, 32:48–52, 34; Numbers 27:12–23; Joshua 1:1–7, 3)

Moses was the first man God chose to lead the Israelites out of their bondage in Egypt. He then led them for forty years on a difficult and problematic journey through the wilderness until they finally arrived on the edge of the Promised Land. It was through Moses that God gave the Israelites the Ten Commandments and the Mosaic Law, found in the first five books of the Bible. During the long journey, Moses prepared a new generation of people to be ready to cross over into the Promised Land. However, he was not able to enter the Promised Land nor did he lead the Israelites into God's Promised Land.

As Moses stood on a mountain looking into the Promised Land, God showed him its beauty and bounty. It was then that God told Moses that he would not be allowed to enter into the Promised Land with the Israelites. It is hard not to sympathize with Moses as he looked at the beauty of the land God had promised, knowing that he could not enter. This is because Moses represents the Old Covenant of the Law, and no one can ever enter the Promised Land by keeping the law. Even though the law is holy and right, it cannot change the sinful nature that is lodged in the heart area of the soul. The law can lead humankind to know their need for a savior but it cannot be the means of salvation.

Joshua is the man God chose to replace Moses. He became the second leader of the Israelites. Joshua was a military leader under Moses and also one of his aides. It was Joshua who was called to lead God's people into the Promised Land. God instructed Joshua to obey Him and all of the laws given to Moses. Joshua did as God instructed, and scripture tells us that he obeyed God completely. It was a new generation of Israelites whom Joshua led into the Promised Land. They did not enter by keeping the law themselves. They entered through Joshua's obedience and by following him.

Joshua is the portrayal of Jesus, the Savior of the world. The name Joshua means "Lord is salvation" or "Yahweh is salvation." The same meaning also applies to the names Jeshua and Jesus. It is Jesus who overcame all the obstacles that stood in the way of humankind's reunion with God in His spiritual-realm kingdom. Jesus answered all the demands of the law, paid the price for the sin of all humankind, and became the only Way to come into the presence of God. In the same way that Joshua led a new generation of Israelites into the Promised Land, Jesus ushered in the New Covenant of Grace for the salvation of humankind.

Saul and David

(Relevant Scriptures: 1 Samuel 9, 10, 31; 2 Samuel 11:26 – 12:13a; Psalms 89:30–37)

It was at the insistence of the Israelites that the Jewish nation received its first human king. They wanted to be like the other nations of the world, with a king of their own to follow. They went to Samuel, a prophet of God, demanding to have a king. Samuel, through prayer, took their request to God. Up until then, God had been their king. The Israelites' demand for a human king was a request to remove God from His rightful position, which was a direct rebellion against His leadership. God instructed Samuel to inform them of the ramifications of having such a king, but nothing Samuel said would sway them. So, God relented and Saul was anointed as the first human king of the Israelites.

Saul did not obey the Lord's instructions and turned out to be exactly the kind of king God foretold. So, God withdrew His anointing from Saul, leaving him as the king of Israel in name only. God then chose David to be His second anointed king of Israel. However, David did not take the throne until after Saul died. Prior to that, David was called to serve King Saul. David became a great warrior, winning many battles for the nation of Israel. He was very popular with the people. Saul became jealous and even tried to kill David, but David would not harm Saul. Saul finally killed himself by falling on his own sword. The Israelites chose David, the man whom God had anointed king years before, as their new king.

The story of Saul and David provides a picture of the relationship between our firstborn, sinful nature and our second, spiritual birth. When the sinful nature entered the soul of humankind, God was forced to depart. Humankind took over God's place of leadership. Saul, the first king of Israel, represents the fall of Adam and Eve, when they made the decision to follow their own desires rather than honor God's leadership. Their decision displaced God from His rightful place and installed themselves on the throne of the human heart. David represents our second decision to give up the throne of our lives and be reunited with the Holy Spirit by accepting Jesus. This biblical account reveals the struggle we go through when determining whom we will follow and allow to have control. Finally, just like Saul, we die to ourselves and give up our seat on the throne of the heart. In so doing, we allow the Holy Spirit to take His rightful place within our hearts. At this stage in our spiritual growth, we make Jesus our Lord as well as the Savior of our soul. It is interesting to note that the Israelites first decided to replace God as their king before they made the second choice to accept the king whom God had anointed to lead them.

As with the other examples, there are different levels of understanding in this story. However, what the Holy Spirit wanted me to understand was that Saul, because of his sin and disobedience, lost God's anointing as king. Although David committed grievous sin in his life, he never lost God's anointing. David experienced God's discipline and suffered the consequences of his sin, but he never lost his anointing or his standing with God. This is because God's covenant with David was an everlasting one, just as the covenant He makes with us through Jesus is an everlasting covenant. The important lesson in this is that the second, spiritual birth never loses God's favor. In our walk with the Lord, we may wander away from Him, fall into sin, and struggle with Him for control. All of these things can disrupt our awareness of the Lord and our communion with Him; however, it cannot separate us from Him. The one thing we cannot do is lose Him, because the moment we accept Jesus as our Savior, our sin is covered by His robe of righteousness and God's Spirit is alive in us, making us always and forever one with Him. One becomes His child of salvation, as well as His child of creation, and there is no way in this world or the next that this can be undone.

Adam and Jesus
(Relevant Scriptures: Romans 5:12–21;
1 Corinthians 15:22, 45–49)

Adam was the first man directly created by God. He had the God-given authority to affect all of creation, so the decisions Adam made, he made for all humanity. It was by directly disobeying God's instruction that Adam and Eve caused all humanity to inherit the sinful nature that is housed in the soul. This created the need for the Spirit of God to depart from the soul of humankind. Scripture describes Jesus as the second Adam. Jesus, like Adam, was directly and uniquely created by God. Like Adam, Jesus had the power and authority to affect all humanity. This made it possible for Jesus to pay the price for the sins of the entire world—past, present, and future. This opened the way for humankind to be reunited with the Spirit of God. It is through Jesus' actions that the sinful nature in us dies and the reunion of our individual spirits with the Holy Spirit is made possible. In other words, through the actions of the first Adam, sin and death became the inheritance of our first birth. Through the actions of Jesus, the second Adam, humanity is freed from the results of the actions of the first Adam and is made spiritually alive in God once again.

There is, however, a difference between how the first Adam and Jesus, the second Adam, carried out their actions. What Adam did immediately became part of the human condition for all of God's children of creation. No one is given the choice to inherit the sinful nature because it is part of the human condition. However, through Jesus' sacrifice, all humankind is given the choice to either confirm or reject the actions of the first Adam and their deadly ramifications. Jesus, the second Adam, presented us with the second choice to either accept or reject God's plan of salvation. When we choose to accept salvation through Jesus, the second Adam, we receive freedom from the inheritance of the first Adam.

There is a reason there is not a blanket salvation that is instantly given to all people and that each individual is given the choice to accept or reject God's plan of salvation. Each individual's choice to accept Jesus, God's everlasting and eternal solution for sin, is an eternal and everlasting decision. Jesus provided the Way for all humanity to become free of the sinful nature and also gave us the choice to be reunited with God's Spirit, allowing us to live in His spiritual kingdom for all eternity. It is because we enter His kingdom by our own decision that God does not ever have to be concerned about another incident like Satan's rebellion against Him in the spiritual realm. This is because all who are in His heavenly kingdom will be totally free of the sinful nature and will have changed hearts devoted to God. Through their own will, they have accepted Jesus as their personal Lord and Savior and crowned Him King of Kings. There will be no more rebellion or turning from God in His kingdom ever again. This is why God created the world, why He covered His spiritual-realm citizens in a body, and why He allows the world to continue until all who would be saved have accepted the only possible way of salvation through Jesus, the second Adam.

***

This natural-realm world is temporal; the spiritual realm is eternal. It is through our first birth that we inherit the sinful nature and our temporary physical life in this natural-realm world. Then, through our second, spiritual birth, we inherit permanent, everlasting, and eternal life in the spiritual realm's kingdom of God. If you have accepted Jesus, then you are alive in the Spirit of God—and that is forever. Salvation comes only from God—not by way of our works, actions, or offerings, but only by being born again. In the above stories, on the physical level, it is evident that God did not hate these men; instead, He provided them with the second birth so that the firstborn could be redeemed and saved. In short, the inheritance of the second birth is everlasting life in the presence of God. It is the fulfillment of God's everlasting covenant with Abraham, which was a covenant of faith. It is through faith in God that the salvation of humankind is accomplished through people's accepting the sacrifice of Jesus, God's Son.

In Closing

(Relevant Scriptures: John 10:28–30; Romans 8:1, 8:35–39; 1 Corinthians 1:8–9, 18–25; 2 Corinthians 1:18–22; 2 Thessalonians 3:3; Jude 24–25)

I know with every fiber of my being that Jesus does not ever eternally lose anyone who has accepted Him as Savior. Jesus is in the business of salvation. I trust with all my heart in the power of what He accomplished on the cross. The apostle Paul writes, "For I am convinced that neither death nor life, neither angel nor demons, neither the present nor the future, nor any powers, neither height nor depth, nor anything else in all creation, will be able to separate us from the love of God that is in Christ Jesus our Lord" (Romans 8:38–39).

How did God convince me that we cannot lose our salvation in Christ? It is through the preponderance of evidence that I have shared in this book. The Holy Spirit has been so gracious to me. His presence and His gifts of revelation have confirmed the truth. I can only conclude that our salvation depends on the power of what Jesus did on the cross. Once an individual has accepted Him, that person is forever in His care. Anything else would suggest that what Jesus did on the cross was not enough or that His strength is not strong enough to keep us. Jude 1:24–25 declares, "To him who is able to keep you from falling and to present you before his glorious presence without fault and with great joy—to the only God our Savior be glory, majesty, power and authority, through Jesus Christ our Lord, before all ages, now and forevermore!" Amen.

Praise God for His magnificent plan!

SOURCES

Chadsey, Charles P., and Harold Wentworth, eds. *The Grosset Webster Dictionary,* revised ed., 1974, s.v. "atonement, believe, cover, forgiveness, fulfill, light, seal."

K., R. "The Unpardonable Sin." *In Touch* 22 (August 2003).

Wiersbe, Warren W. "Philippians 2 Chapter 5." *The Bible Exposition Commentary* vol. 2. Wheaton, IL: Victor, 1989.

Wiersbe, Warren W. "Mark 3-4 Chapter 3." *The Bible Exposition Commentary* vol. 1 Wheaton, IL: Victor, 1989.

Saint Augustine. "Saint Augustine Quotes." *BrainyQuotes.* N.p., n.d. Web. 14 July 2014.

Joyner, Rick. "The Two Trees." *There Were Two Trees in the Garden.* Pineville: Morning Star Publications, 1986. 7. Print.

Smith, Dr. William, comp. "Death." Def. 1 and 2. *Smith's Bible Dictionary.* Revised ed. Philadelphia: A. J. Holman, n.d. 73. Print.